Get Clean

By
Jams N. Roses

Copyright © 2016 Jams N. Roses

This book is a work of fiction, names characters, places and incidents are the product of the author's imagination. Any resemblance to actual events, places or persons, living or dead, is coincidental.

No part of this publication may be reproduced, distributed, transmitted or stored in a database in any form, without the prior permission of the publisher.

This book shall not be lent, resold, hired out or otherwise circulated without the publisher's prior consent.

Published by Jams N. Roses 2016
All rights reserved.
ISBN: 1492886491
ISBN-13:9781492886495

DEDICATION

For Mani Lee,
My pride, my joy, my golden boy.

Brief Comment

For legal reasons, I cannot claim all the events described in this book are true. But some of them are. Enough to make me cringe when reading it back. Enjoy.

An addict, a psychopath, a drug dealer and his girlfriend. This is a story of addiction, bad decisions and terrible friends. Before we can pick ourselves up, we must sometimes hit rock bottom.

Split

1 - FRIENDS

So there I was, Jimmy Walker, on my last night out with the boys, marking the end of one chapter, and the beginning of another.

I sat at the same table, at the same pub, surrounded by the same friends, drinking the same drinks and talking the same drunken nonsense we'd been talking for as long as I can remember.

Habits, we're creatures of habit, us humans, some more than others.

It wasn't long before Scott offered me a line of Cocaine, or 'Trumpet,' as he preferred to call it. Although I was feeling a little tipsy, I'd made a promise to myself that I wouldn't be doing any more of those little white lines, so I declined. Sure, it had been one of many promises I'd made concerning that moreish Colombian export, but at some point you've got to just say no, like those kids from Grange Hill (although I have heard a few of them were a little self-indulgent, at times).

'Come on, Jimbo,' said Tommy, sliding a small, round tablet along the table and tucking it away behind my drink, 'this'll get you in the mood. It's your last night with the boys, mate, get involved.'

'Bastards,' I thought.

GET CLEAN

Why is it that some people always find themselves spending time, even wasting time, with people that really aren't pulling in the same direction?

I took a gulp of lager, washing down a dose of ecstasy as I did so. I felt the familiar lump of synthetic enjoyment bump its way to the back of my mouth, down my throat and into the pit of my stomach, only to feel it work its way into my bloodstream, up from my feet, through my legs and body and down my arms before pulling my cheeks apart and forcing a smile on my face within minutes.

'So how long d'you reckon you'll stay in Spain then, mate?' asked Lee.

'He'll be back in three weeks, tail between his legs, begging for a couch to sleep on!' interjected Dave, always the loudest of the group. He managed to get a laugh on this occasion as well.

Little did they know that there was a part of me that did worry about failing completely on my new adventure at the first obstacle, and having to come back and swallow the abuse that these guys would thoroughly enjoy dishing out to me.

I tilted my head back against the wall, and gave Scott a nudge with my elbow.

'I wouldn't mind that upper now, mate.'

I followed Scott into the men's room.

We walked past one of the old alcoholics who was pissing into a urinal, or at least had been at some point, and had near-enough fallen asleep whilst standing with his head pressed against the cold wall tiles. We stepped into the same toilet cubicle, locking the door behind us. If the old boy had noticed us was debatable, but sadly irrelevant too.

Between us, and all the others who took drugs on a regular basis like us, thousands and thousands of lines of Coke must've been 'racked up' on the toilets in this pub. Fat lines, thin lines, long lines and those ridiculously short lines you get given when whoever's got the Charlie isn't feeling overly generous; an end of the night at the end of the month kind of situation.

No more cash, no more Coke, may as well go home then.

But it wasn't one of them nights, far from it, in fact. Scott had taken to buying 'eighths' at a time nowadays, three and a half grams, with the purpose of it lasting longer, and his money going further. But it never worked out like that.

One problem with Cocaine, as many a user can testify, is that when you start, stopping is a really difficult thing to do. In fact, after your first line, then your sixth and seventh line, stopping isn't really an option anymore. It almost seems like a bad idea.

In my opinion, this isn't the 'long term addiction' that'll get you robbing your neighbours or even your family so as you can afford to buy your next hit, it's just that while you have the drug flowing through your blood, you are constantly chasing the high it gave you during those first minutes.

With Cocaine, the high really doesn't last that long, not for the price, certainly. Thankfully, after a good night's sleep and a good feed, this 'short term addiction' wears off and you become yourself again, forgetting that line sniffing, snot dribbling, Coke monster until the next time you decide to, or can afford to, get high again.

As Scott tipped out enough Trumpet for a 'proper' line each, almost perfectly measured by eye, like an old-school cocktail barman who refuses to use the optical measures out of professional pride, I took out the first note I came across from my pocket and began to roll it into a straw-like object, until I noticed that the fiver was old and a bit flimsy, so I changed it for a newer twenty-pound note that was crisp and more practical for the job in hand.

'So, you're really going through with this?' Scott asked.

'Yeah, man,' I replied, 'I just need to get away, you know.'

'And you're sure this ain't 'coz Colleen got with that mug from Watford? It won't last, mate.'

He took the makeshift straw and sniffed up his line up Coke in one, short, powerful sniff, then handed it back to me.

'Listen, Scott, you know it got me down. But she left me before he came along. She left me because I drink too much and I'm half a Coke-head who's going nowhere in life. And we both know the misery she's been through because of me.'

I rubbed my left nostril and snorted, clearing any obstacles my nose might've had concealed that could potentially block my line of happiness from reaching its destination. Then I leant forward and cleared the tiled surface of Powder.

'I don't blame her for leaving me, and she's not the reason I'm leaving here,' I continued.

And what I told him was true, pretty much.

The thought of running into the love of my life with her new man, was definitely something I was keen to avoid. It had only been a couple of months since the last time I'd broken down in tears over the whole episode. But more than that, I'm a junkie. Maybe not a heroin addict, or a meth-head, but most of my money goes on drink and drugs, and smoking of course, which isn't getting any cheaper. Then there's the hangovers as well, I swear they get worse week by week. Seriously, I only feel fully recovered from a weekend by the Thursday, and then there's only one day of normality before I'm handing over more money to the barman, drug dealer or tobacconist.

To say my work had suffered was an understatement. I really couldn't stand being there anymore, and they didn't want me either, so when I handed in my notice it was a happy day for everyone.

Scott pissed into the toilet as I unrolled my money and shoved it deep into my pocket. We left the cubicle and washed our hands, I cooled my face and my balding head with some of the cold water as Scott touched his hair whilst staring into the mirror.

'And this job, what's the crack exactly?' he asked.

'It's selling property, or timeshare, or something like that,' I replied, a little embarrassed at the fact I didn't know exactly what I was going to be doing in Spain. 'It's not important, anyway. I just need a change of scene. I want a change of scene. It'll do me good, you know?'

He nodded, maybe in thoughtful agreement,

maybe because he didn't know what to say. But then he did say something.

'So you're gonna come back a changed man,' he stated, hopefully.

I smiled.

I liked the thought of that, coming back a changed man, no longer having to shoulder the weight of being an underachiever, to come back a winner, and proud, and happy, and drug-free.

'It's like you can read my mind, Scott.'

'I've just known you too long, mate.'

We high-fived, then for some reason he gave me a hug. Maybe he was sad to see me go, but more likely he was incredibly high and we all get a bit soft when we're steaming.

'Worst case scenario, you'll be back in three weeks like that muppet out there said,' he said.

'Is this a private party?' asked Dave.

Scott let me go and we turned to see Dave's head stuck through the men's room door.

'And who you calling a muppet?' he continued. 'Come on girls, finish your cuddle, we got a line of Sambuca's on the bar.'

We had our shots, then more beers, then more shots, and so on. Occasionally we'd visit the men's room for business as usual and we were just having a good time. Good fun, bad jokes and the occasional rejection from below average women.

We were all sat back at the table watching Tommy, who stood at the bar with a couple of heavily made-up teenagers, borderline illegal drinkers, when Dave piped up.

'Boys, watch,' he said, before vomiting into his

pint glass, then continuing to drink from it, and then stating as a matter of fact, 'I'm a fucking legend.'

Lee covered his mouth in horror as me and Scott creased up in laughter. Tommy had noticed from the bar and tried his best to look like he didn't know us, which didn't work for long as Scott stood up and joined him and the two girls.

Tommy bowed his head, shamefully, as Scott whispered into the ears of the blondest of the two blondes, who reacted swiftly with a hasty slap across his face. She grabbed her friend by the arm and they both left. Scott laughed and apologised to Tommy, who shrugged it off as standard behaviour and gulped down the rest of his beer.

I wouldn't change them for the world, my friends. It's me that has got to change.

'I'll enjoy tonight, but from tomorrow I'll be the new me. The new improved, sensible, sober, happy me who achieves things and makes his family and friends proud,' I thought to myself, before I sneaked off to the toilet, locked the door on the cubicle, sank to my knees and puked.

2 - FAMILY

The four of us were sat around the small dining table at the back of the living room. My sister, Esther, and her son, Finley, had joined me and my mum, Charlotte, for a roast dinner.

Esther was a good looking woman, a few years older than me, but a little tired looking from the stress of bringing up her boy on her own. Finley was great though, and you could see the bond between them was something special, even if he did test her patience at times.

'Thanks mum,' said Esther, 'that was great,' as she laid her knife and fork down on her empty plate.

'It was more of a team effort, to be honest' mum replied, smiling at me.

'Then thank you, too, James' she said, ever so slightly sarcastically, knowing by the clear signs of a hangover written all over me, that I likely played a very small part in the preparation of any food.

'No problem.'

Finley used his knife to roll around the remains of his dinner, which was all his vegetables, as me and my mum finished what was left on our plates.

'Finish your food,' Esther snapped at Finley, bored at having the same situation play out whenever he didn't fancy eating the healthy part of his meals.

My mum stood and stacked her, mine and Esther's plates then took them out to the kitchen.

'Hey Jimmy,' called Finley, 'look.'

I looked to my side and saw my nephew using a stick of carrot to simulate smoking a cigarette.

'Eat your bloody food, Finley,' Esther snapped, 'or you'll get no dessert. I mean it.'

Esther was stressed more than usual today. Partly due to me leaving, I think, worrying about the trouble I may get into whilst away, without her or my mum being there to bail me out of trouble. But also she was worried about mum, who was really worried about me. There was a giant vacuum of worry circulating and it seemed to be entirely my fault. Which to be honest, it was.

'This is killing her, you know?' A statement and question all rolled into one.

I nodded, with a slight shrug of my shoulders to boot. What could I say? I felt like I needed this, and my mum and Esther were meant to be the strong ones, how come I'm the only person who didn't seem to think my trying pastures new is a bad idea? Other than Finley, of course, my darling nephew who thinks the proverbial sun shines from my backside, bless him.

'Have you decided how long you'll be away yet?' she asked, 'I can't be here all the time checking on her, I've got this little brat to look after. This better not be just some extended boys holiday.'

'It isn't.'

'Always drinking, and shoving that shit up your nose.'

'Mummy, you swore!' said Finley, giggling away at his mum's loss of control.

'Quiet, Finley,' she said, turning her attention to the apple of her eye, 'take your plate out to your nan.'

'But I haven't finished my vegetables,' he answered.

'Just take your plate to nanny and ask for a bowl of ice-cream.'

Finley slipped down off his chair, picked up his plate, walked around the table, and gave me a wink when Esther wouldn't have been able to see. I love my nephew, cheeky little sod that he is.

'Listen, Es, I know I got problems. I know it'll upset mum, me not being here. And I know I gotta get off the gear, once and for all,' I said, truthfully and open-hearted, as is the only way when speaking to someone who knows you better than you know yourself, 'but to do that, I need a change of scenery. I need to get away from here. Like a fresh start, even if just for a couple of months.'

I think Esther knew deep down that it wasn't a completely bonkers idea, drastic action to cause a drastic change. The craziness of it almost made it seem like a good idea, the more I thought about it, anyway.

'Just, as long as you sort yourself out, James.'

She reached across the table and placed her hands on mine, a big sister who has seen her little brother make more than his fair share of mistakes, and looked me straight in the eyes, to give me another one of those serious messages that she'd have to convey to me every now and again in my life.

'Get clean, James. Just, get clean.'

Esther and Finley had left not long after eating, the day was drawing to a close and lately she was enforcing Finley's bedtime as never before, adamant that showing him who's boss would give him a bit of stability, and maybe a bit of direction in life at a later date. It crossed my mind that this was the sort of disciplined upbringing that we lacked as kids, although I didn't say anything to her or mum, of course. Besides, Esther turned out alright, so it would be unfair to put any blame on my mum for my shortfalls.

I had just finished doing the washing-up when mum entered the kitchen and put a dirty cup on the sideboard. Why is there always something that appears just as you are drying your hands?

Mum rested her head on my shoulder as I washed up the cup and dried my hands again on the tea-towel.

'So you've got everything packed, and you know where your passport is?' She asked, again.

'Yes, mum, for the third time,' I said, 'all packed, passport ready and cash changed up.'

I put the tea-towel to the side and turned to face her; I could see the sadness and worry on her face.

'I just don't want you stressing out later when things aren't where they're supposed to be,' she said, putting her arms around me and pulling me close, 'and your tablets, did you get to the doctor's for more tablets?'

'No, mum,' I replied, 'I've stopped the tablets. I wanna try and do this on my own.'

I love my mum, although if you knew half the shit that I'd put her through these last few years, you'd be forgiven for thinking otherwise. She's always been there for me, wasted the last of her savings on unsuccessfully putting me through rehab, had me crying on her shoulder through bouts of depression, and was even the one who found me when I overdosed. I must be draining the life out of her; nobody deserves a break like my old dear.

Going away wasn't just for me.

'It's not too late to change your mind and stay,' she said, 'You don't have to go through with this.'

'Mum, I've quit my job, given up the flat and sold my car. It's a bit late to be getting cold feet, don't you think?'

'I'm just worried about you being all the way out there by yourself.'

'I know you are. But I don't want you to worry about me, I want you to start looking after yourself, do some things that you wanna do, for you, you know?'

I stepped back from mum's embrace and held her gently by the arms, looking into her eyes, and seeing the pain and torture in her soul.

'I won't be gone forever, and when I'm back, I'll be back for good.'

I let go and slowly made my way to the door towards the hallway and stairs.

'I'm gonna go and pack a few last bits then hit the sack,' I said, and then turned to see her standing over the sink, wiping a tear from her cheek.

I rested my head against the doorframe and

breathed out a gentle sigh. Nobody likes to see their mother suffer the way that she was clearly suffering, but I was the cause of the suffering, and knew that some time away from this sorry excuse for a life that I had built for myself would be a good thing for me, and ultimately a good thing for her, to see me come through it and shine like the younger me that made her proud and gave her the happiness that I see in her eyes when she is playing with Finley.

'I'll wake you up before I leave in the morning, mum.'

I left her standing at the sink, no doubt about to examine the washing up I just did, not knowing that I knew she always checked the job I'd done, and Esther's too when she'd done it. Sometimes she'd redo a few bits. Did she really think we couldn't take being told our washing up wasn't up to scratch? I think maybe she thought we'd think she was a bit obsessive compulsive if she admitted it. She really was a little fragile; I'm glad that Esther and Finley would be here when I'm gone, because otherwise this personal project of mine wouldn't have been an option.

3 – TAKE OFF

I was nervous all morning. I had a tight, uncomfortable feeling in the pit of my stomach as I said goodbye to mum, it persisted as Lee drove me to the airport and even a coffee and cigarette followed by a visit to the toilets didn't ease the feeling. It was nerves all right. I had sweat trickling down my forehead at the thought of getting on that plane and saying goodbye to everyone and everything I had ever known, without any real clue as to what might lie ahead.

At this point, I should probably say that I'd never been to Marbella, on the south coast of Spain. I'd never even been to Spain before, except a lad's holiday to Ibiza, but I'm not sure if that really counts.

I'd found my new job on the internet, and the company helped with relocation and gave a basic wage that you could survive on and was available to start as and when I was good and ready. I thought it sounded a bit too good to be true, but justified to it myself as a good performance by me in the group interview, and also that not everybody was brave enough or prepared to just up and leave everything to try something new in someplace far from family and friends.

I'd reread an email from MacArthur Realty

International, my new employers, the night before I left whilst struggling to sleep, and used a couple of the links they'd supplied to find out a bit about the town where I'd be working and the 'endless opportunities of financial gain and career enhancement' I'd have at my disposal, whilst employed by the 'number one company on the coast.'

Sat on the plane, I was talking to a guy who had a place not far from where I was heading, apparently. I'd soon found out that the Costa Del Sol was home to a lot of property investment companies, the next generation of hard-sell companies after the bottom fell out of the timeshare market. I didn't like the sound of this, I wasn't told about hard-selling in the interview, I didn't even know what hard-selling was really, and selling of any sort didn't really appeal, to be honest. I thought I was booking holidays for people, or similar, maybe this guy was talking about something else, got his wires crossed or something.

I collected my bag from the carousel at Malaga airport and walked outside towards the taxi rank, the heat and exhaust fumes hit me hard.

'Marbella Centro, Café Marbella,' I said, wondering how useful those weekly Spanish lessons I'd been doing for the last month and a half would prove to be.

It was about a half hour drive from the airport to Marbella.

'This place is beautiful,' I thought to myself as the taxi driver weaved in and out of the traffic, heading west along the two-lane, coastal road.

No cloud dared try and share the sun's blue sky. The sea, a stone throw to my left, was calm and inviting, even if I was never the best swimmer, and had an irrational fear of sharks ever since seeing Jaws at perhaps too young an age. Do they get sharks in the Mediterranean Sea? I'd have to look into that before swim-suiting up and taking the plunge.

I was feeling more relaxed at this point. I guess that the warm air, blue sky and the 'endless opportunities' I had in front of me had settled my nerves. Until, that is, I arrived at Café Marbella, the meeting point for all the new MacArthur recruits.

I introduced myself to Karen, who wore a company uniform, carried a clipboard and also an air of self-importance, as 'James' not 'Jimmy'. I felt that this made me seem more mature, a quality that I'd definitely lacked recently. She told me she was the head of human resources, and was nice enough to inform me I was the last one to arrive and that everybody had been waiting for me.

As I glanced over her shoulder, I felt my stomach go again.

I'd dressed in joggers and hooded top, with the aim of being comfortable during the flight. Ironically, the clothes that I wore were at this point the reason I felt incredibly uncomfortable; all seven of the other new starters were wearing suit and tie, or the female equivalent. A couple of them had noticed my late arrival and lack of self-presentation skills, and chuckled to themselves whilst delicately stubbing out their cigarettes and sipping from their ridiculously small coffee cups.

I knew right then, at that very moment, the

type of people that usually would give up everything and everyone they know to travel someplace new for 'endless opportunities of financial gain and career enhancement,' sales people.

And I fucking hate sales people. In my experience, all salesmen are overly alpha-male, two-faced snakes. And saleswomen, well, the less said about those devious, money-hungry sluts, the better.

Karen and two of her staff, also wearing the company colours, ushered me and my new colleagues into three BMW's and took us to our places of residence, a collection of studio and one and two bedroom apartments just outside of the main town. I'd been told that I would be staying in a studio on my own, which was fine by me, almost a blessing I thought. Having to bunk up with one of these guys would have been awkward, I would have been found out to be far from the salesman I'd sold myself as during the interview. Or is that a paradox, of sorts? I'd sold myself, so, perhaps I am capable?

As I sat between the suited and booted, talking about how much money they had earned before and will earn here, whilst being driven along in the nice car, in the sunshine by the sea, it was hard not to start believing the hype, hard not to have that little bit of hope that maybe this was the start of something great about to happen in my life. I was surrounded by people who truly believed that they were 'the business,' and had landed jobs with the 'number one company on the coast,' and I had been chosen as well.

'Maybe I do belong here?'

Two weeks had passed, and me and the group, sixteen of us newbies in total, all now suited and booted, had been through some pretty intensive training.

We had been educated about the housing market, which was apparently the only viable investment option for the average Joe. We were taught about the company we worked for, how the owner and founder of MacArthur Realty International, a certain Darragh MacArthur, had started the company with only eight thousand pounds of his own money, and built it up from scratch. We were taught the best way to gain the trust of our potential clients, using the name of Mr MacArthur as a guarantee to the quality of our portfolios and investment advice. We were even shown how to show the public that would be coming to see us how to use the equity in their current properties to fund an overseas investment.

It all seemed so simple, too good an opportunity to miss. I even thought about trying to scrape together a few grand to put into property.

I discovered my job would be phoning people who had enquired via the company website, or answering calls from those who called in after watching our infomercials on MRI's new television channel, and book them on a trip to the location that they were interested in buying a property in.

It was that simple.

I wouldn't be selling, per sé, but giving information about our company, answering any questions and getting credit card details to book flights for a meeting between the buyers and our reps on the ground. I was told our reps were the best in the business, and would close eight out of ten potential deals. Our salesmen were so good, apparently, that we were discouraged from selling any off-plan properties over the phone. The logic was if someone is willing to put down a deposit on one unit, without even visiting the location, then how many units could our highly-trained sales team get the investors to purchase?

I would get a percentage of any units sold that followed my booking of the sales trip.

'Easy as pie.'

Almost everyone had believed everything that we had been taught. We had been told over and over the same facts and seen the figures and watched the presentations that at the end of it, you would be a fool not to believe in the product. It had everyone sucked into it, everyone except my new Australian buddy, Jason Dorris.

'Well that's it guys and girls. These two weeks should have prepared you for the "boiler room." You know what you've got to do, and on Monday you'll be expected to do it. This will be your last weekend off until the end of the season, so make the most of it' said Lorna, the head trainer for new staff.

Jason stood and punched the air.

'Alright, let's get on it' he said, excitedly.

Me and a few of the others stood to leave but were directed to sit back down again by Lorna. I'd noticed that every member of staff with an ounce of authority felt the need to act like an arsehole.

'Stay seated,' she said, 'Remember; you are now ambassadors for this company. If anybody gets into any sort of trouble that could reflect badly on the reputation of this company, I will personally kick you out onto Beach-bum Avenue. Understand?'

'Yes, mam,' said Jason, under his breath, which was pretty well restrained for him.

Lorna left the room and Jason turned to me, a massive grin slapped across his face.

'Right, let's get on it, Jimbo,' he said, 'Are you coming to the port or what?'

What else was I going to do? Like Lorna said, it was the last weekend we'd have off until the end of the season, whenever that was.

'Yeah, fuck it,' I replied, 'I'm not having a mad one though.'

'Cool. I'll meet you out front in a couple of hours; I gotta go and meet our mate, "Charlie."'

'You're getting Charlie? Again?' I asked, a little shocked, although I shouldn't have been shocked at all.

Back home, the Cocaine was strictly a weekend thing. But here, in the bars and pubs, you could see it on the faces of lots of people no matter what time of the day, or day of the week. Jason was as bad as anyone I'd ever met for it, but he functioned well on it, not missing work once and hiding his eyes behind his shades when he was really on one.

'Just a couple of bags, you know how it is. I'll see you around eight tonight. Hey, did you want a bag for yourself?' He asked, ever the gentleman.

'No, that's alright mate, cheers.'

'Yeah, whatever, man. You say that now, then after a couple of beers you'll be chewing my ear off to give you some like the other night,' he said, 'I'll bring you one just in case.'

And with that, he gave me a wink and left, like a little tornado off to cause mayhem elsewhere.

Jason had come to Spain to hook up with some Spanish chick, Lourdes, who he met whilst travelling around India. Within two days of getting here, he found her screwing her ex-boyfriend, Pedro, and proceeded to beat two tons of crap out of them using an iron. Generally, a foreigner coming into town and beating on locals is not the thing to do, but Jason didn't give a fuck. He left the east coast town and found himself in Marbella, courtesy of a bit of labouring work he landed with another Australian he'd met in a bar. The other guy had since long gone, and Jason now lived with an English woman in town, but he hadn't really said too much on that subject, except when high he'd let slip a few details.

He's a good laugh and we got on well, but he's a live one.

If I wasn't feeling so lonely when work had finished, I probably would have avoided Jason, what with my goal of getting clean and all. But he played it down, the Cocaine, and said he'd tell me straight if he thought I had a real problem.

'A few beers, a few lines, nobody's gonna die,' he'd say.

'Well, if nobody's gonna die,' I'd say.

4 – JASON AND SARAH

Jason went home to get changed, maybe have a wash and a bite to eat, but more importantly for him, to get some Powder.

He scored it off his landlady, Sarah, not that she was a dealer, but her boyfriend was, and it was easier for Jason to deal with her, because the Moroccan didn't think much of him. Apparently it was the best he'd ever had on the coast. I hadn't met either Sarah or Amine, but had a hunch the problem between the two men was Jason living under the same roof as Amine's girlfriend.

It's a bit complicated, because from what I gathered, Amine didn't want to commit to Sarah, but didn't want to let her go either. She wanted to be with Amine, but was reaching the point of accepting that marriage was a long way off, and that maybe she just had to wait until he was ready.

Jason said she liked having a man around the house, but made it clear there wasn't anything naughty going on between him and Sarah, although from how he talked about her, I guess he'd like to give her more than just the rent each month.

Sarah was an attractive, black woman, in her early thirties, sexy, but with a touch of class about her. She wore designer clothes, with hair and nails done to perfection. Not that Jason had told me this, and we hadn't met at this point, I had to wait until we met for the first time to see how gorgeous she was. If Amine is as dangerous as Jason hints he is, then not cracking onto his bird would be a smart thing to do, which maybe explains why Jason is always out of the apartment, getting drunk or high, anything but putting himself in the line of fire.

'So, did you see your man earlier?' asked the tenant.

'I did,' replied Sarah, not bothering to look up from her magazine, 'Your bits are above the microwave in the brown cup.'

'I'm gonna take an extra one for a mate, ok?'

'No problem. Just leave the money in the cup.'

Jason went to the kitchen, grabbed the brown cup and fished out three bags of Cocaine, each containing around a gram of the Class A drug. I say 'around a gram,' as unless you check each bag you buy, you never really know how much there is. Also, if you do check every bag you buy, you know that you never actually get a full gram. He counted out one hundred and eighty euros, folded it up then put it into the cup and placed it back on the shelf it came from.

Jason checked his hair in the mirror and put his sunglasses on, then made his way back to the front room. He stood at the door, not saying a word, just watching Sarah read her magazine.

She must have felt his gaze drilling into her and looked up at him.

'What is it?' she asked.

'Oh, did you have any news for me, about that

other thing?'

'No, not yet, I told you it'd probably be a few more weeks.'

'Ok, cool. And, well, I just wondered how you were doing. You know, is everything alright?' Jason enquired, 'I heard you arguing again on the phone last night, just worried about you, that's all.'

Sarah closed the magazine.

'Yes, Jason, everything is fine. Now, if you don't mind, I just want to relax a bit before I go to work. Ok?'

'Yeah, sure, that's cool,' he said, hiding any pain from what was clearly a rejection. 'But remember; don't work hard, work smart.'

He gave her his cheesy grin, winked and then left.

5 - PROSPECTS

Jason and I sat at a table on the terrace of an English bar, overlooking the port and the beautiful sea. There were others from work at the bar, but as usual, we chose to sit apart from the crowd. They were still wearing their suits and sporting ray-ban sunglasses and trying to outdo each other with tales of money made, women dated and professional positions held.

By contrast, we were dressed down and slurring our words. We'd had a few beers quite rapidly, and were both high as kites.

'I knew you couldn't resist the Powder,' stated Jason, smugly.

Was I a victim of peer pressure? Maybe.

Jason was certainly an enabler. Although, if he hadn't had brought the Cocaine from home, scoring some whilst out and about in Marbella wasn't difficult at all. If you couldn't get some from whichever bar you were in, maybe you'd have to venture to the bar next door, or at a stretch, to the bar the other side of the street or a two minute walk around the block.

Jason was loud when he spoke, more so after a beer and some of 'The Other', so I tried to change the subject from anything illegal, for fear of being asked to leave what was actually a nice little boozer in a good location.

'So what do you think of this place then, Jase?' I asked. 'You've been here a while.'

'This place fucking rocks mate,' he answered enthusiastically, 'I can't wait to get my new bar job, earn some big money.'

'New bar job?' I thought. 'What's he talking about now?'

'What do you mean? Why've you just done two weeks of training if you're gonna go for another job straight away?'

'The bar doesn't get busy for another week or so,' he said, 'My landlady's gonna help me get an interview with the boss there, so I got to do this shit until it's sorted, keep her off my back.'

'Really?' I asked, 'This was just about killing time for you?'

'Jimbo, one, being ordered around by them cunts, and two, wearing a fucking suit?' he counted off his two best reasons on his fingers. 'This ain't for me mate. If I was wearing that suit back in Melbourne I'd be shot! Fucking red-necks would have a field day!'

When Jason spoke, he was crude, almost backward sounding, but he did usually have a good point, which he was never shy in sharing. Honestly, if he did decide to go into the property sales profession, he'd not be too bad if he toned down the language a bit. But it seems he's got other ideas.

'Yeah, I see what you mean.' I said, thoughtfully. 'I guess it's almost army-like, with the shouting orders, the dress-code.' I'd just counted off on my fingers my two best reasons for agreeing with him.

'D'you think it'll be as bad now that training has finished?' I continued.

Jason toked on a cigarette and took a gulp from his beer, shaking his head as he placed his glass back onto the table and flicked ash on the floor.

'It's gonna get worse. You speak to half of the English or Irish working behind the bars out here, they've all done it. Tell me Jimbo, why are you here?' he asked.

This wasn't the first time he'd asked me a serious question. Cocaine does that to people, makes you get all soppy, even if just for a minute or two, and you feel like an agony aunt for someone and you want to help solve any problems that they may or may not have, give them career advice, as Jason was about to do to me.

'The experience? The money?' he continued.

'Well, I've never had a job where you can earn what you can earn here, so, the money, I guess,' I said, unconvincingly, even to myself.

'And you think you'll earn what they say?' he said, that grin spread across his face. 'Even if you earned it, do you think you'll get everything they owe you? Oh, Jimbo.'

It was my turn to smoke, he was making me nervous.

'What the fuck are you talking about?'

'You'll get your basic, which ain't much, but commission? You'd better be prepared to wait, mate. Besides, how many of these firms have folded in the last couple years? Nearly all of them, I'd say.'

'What? You reckon?' I said, realising at this point, that anybody listening into our conversation could see that I was a fish out of water, a million miles from home and no clue what I was really doing here.

'I'm serious, Jimbo, ask anyone,' said the wise Australian. 'Plus, you're not protected by unions and shit like where you're from. I tell you, there's only one way to make real money out here, and it's the same as every other country you've been to.'

I didn't have to ask what. I knew that as soon as he'd finished stubbing out that cigarette, then maybe taking another swig of beer, that he was going to share his magnificent knowledge with me, the information that was going to open my eyes and make everything become so clear to clueless me.

For the first time, after numerous occasions of being out in public with Jason, he glanced at the clientele around us, and leant across the table in order to say something he didn't want everyone else to hear.

'Selling drugs mate. Believe me, it's where the money is, on this coast especially. You wanna know why?' he asked.

'Great one, make money by selling drugs, a little cliché,' I thought.

'Tell me,' I said.

'Everybody does it. Look around. Take a look around and see with your own eyes, Coke-heads, all of 'em, even us for fuck's sake. Everyone's on it.'

When you are high on drugs, it's like everybody is high on drugs. It's an assumption, a deluded reasoning brought to fruition due to the drugs that you yourself are high on.

But, at the same time, it is hard to say that people aren't high. It was incredibly easy to score Cocaine here, probably easier to get than marijuana even. The Coke was certainly better than that in England and cheaper too.

And there was a lot of money here, 'disposable income,' even if not in our profession as Jason had just informed me. There were nice cars, nice boats, men dressed well with gorgeous women on their arms, eating in fine looking restaurants and drinking in wine bars, smoking expensive cigars. You could easily picture these people living the 'high' life, if you'll forgive the pun.

'So, how come you aren't serving up then, Jase?' I asked, curiously.

He winked at me.

'I will be. I got a plan. I'll get this bar job sussed, work out who runs what, then pow! I'll have the Coke-heads queuing up to score. You wait and see.'

'So, you're here for the money as well then, Jase?'

'I am now, and getting high, drunk and fucking chicks!'

'I'll drink to that,' I said.

We both raised our glasses, and then Jason downed the rest of his whilst I just took a sip of mine.

In all honesty, his revelations about the property industry had brought me down a bit, I'd have to ask about and see how much he had been saying was true. I'd kind of fallen hook, line and sinker with all the talk about earning big, selling glamourous properties and even helping strangers invest their hard earned cash into feasible projects and becoming a little richer with the help of my newly found expertise.

Had I just been mis-sold a dream?

'You know what?' he said, 'you English ain't too bad are you?'

'Best race in the world mate.'

'Whatever you say, Jimbo, whatever you say. But I'll tell you something for nothing right now.'

'What's that?'

Jason slammed his empty glass on the table and pointed a finger at me, holding it no more than two inches from my face. It smelled of tobacco and ash.

'It's your fucking round! Back in a sec, I'm going for a piss.'

That was one sentence he didn't mind sharing with the rest of the bar.

I finished my drink and sparked another cigarette. Cocaine made me smoke more than usual, sometimes I'd go a day without a cigarette, but after a line it's like a switch has been flicked and I can't get enough nicotine into my system. Another bad 'high habit' was that I always rubbed the end of my nose, for two reasons, which are, Cocaine makes your nose run, and you can also get a bit paranoid about little white flakes of the expensive Powder fallen and becoming visible to those around you. Both of these are unattractive to look at, especially to the fairer sex.

Suddenly, Jason ran out of the toilet and back to the table.

'We gotta go,' he said, as he shoved his cigarettes back into his pocket.

'What you doing?' I asked.

'Toilets,' he said, gesturing with his head to the toilet door he had just run from.

I looked over to see an old man stumbling through the door, blood all over his England football shirt.

'I thought you said the English were alright?' I said, making a joke at a most inappropriate time.

'He was looking at my cock,' said Jason, shoving his phone and lighter into a pocket. 'You coming or not?'

I left a twenty euros note on the table to cover our bill and we left, jogging light-footedly along the promenade.

'Fucking hell, Jase, you can't behave yourself,' I thought, not for the first time.

6 – THE BOILER ROOM

It was a week into the 'boiler room' that things started to fall apart for me and my real estate investment advisory career.

We'd all been working hard on the telephones for nine hours a day. Now some people might not think that sitting or standing by a desk for nine hours is hard labour, but it sure as shit isn't easy. I've been rejected by quite a few women in my life, some that I've cared for, others less important, but the constant rejection you receive as a telemarketer pushes you to the limit. I'd been threatened, verbally abused, laughed at, had people just hang up the phone and even one guy who cried. And personally, I don't blame my 'potential clients.'

Our leads were regurgitated from exhibition shows that happened anywhere from a month to five years ago. There were notes on the files with times and dates from previous telemarketers who had tried and failed to book these 'investors' on a viewing trip. Some of the notes were funny, 'Said to stop phoning as all money had been lost in Vegas, so take her name off the list', 'Said can't talk now, call back when you've got a proper job', and my personal favourite, 'Said to stop calling or would fucking shoot me.'

This last lead was dated just a week ago, so I made up a note, 'no answer,' and put it onto the 'no booking' pile. At the end of today's shift I'd put these leads back into the administration office, who would then give them to the next guy when he had gone through the leads he had last been given.

It was an awful exercise for everybody involved.

Mr MacArthur refused to accept that the leads were no good, his logic being that the contact details were given by an interested party at some point, and we would keep trying them until the interested party was in a position that needed our specialised services. Another argument was that the telemarketer just didn't build a good enough rapport with the future client, so it was always worth another attempt from a new telemarketer.

I was working next to Jason, which kind of made the days bearable.

Remember I said that Jason would make a good salesman? Well, maybe if he actually gave a shit. I assume his head wasn't really into it, and he was just biding his time until the bar job came through, as he was truly impolite to some of these people. Normally I'm not keen on rudeness to people that don't deserve it, but the stress of the job, and the abuse I'd received from my own phone calls, made it a little more acceptable when Jason flirted outrageously with the females, and was downright rude to the men.

Arguing with people wouldn't get you a booking, but it did build up your phone minutes, which were monitored by the office manager,

Richard Robinson, or Robbo as he liked to be known.

Me and Jason hadn't booked or sold a thing by the way, like most of the guys in that office. This job was hard, slow and painful. I hated salesmen before, and now I hated them even more, regardless if I was one or not.

'Yes sir, I appreciate that, but if you... Well, all I need is five minutes... Well that's not a very nice thing to say, sir. I'm just doing my job and... You've hung up' I spoke into the phone, before turning my attention to Jason's latest business call.

'Who do you think you're talking to, buddy? No, no you listen to me... No, fuck you,' he said, before slamming down the receiver.

At this point, we had given up all attempts to remain professional, and learnt to laugh at our shortcomings at MacArthur Realty International.

'I don't think I'm getting the hang of this,' said Jason.

'Tell me about it,' I said.

'Well, at least you'd listen.'

'Oi,' called out Robbo.

He strutted out of his glass-walled office at the end of the room, chest out and red faced as he exhaled the smoke from his menthol cigarette.

'Hang up the phones and come 'ere,' he barked.

All eighty of us telemarketers gathered at Robbo's end of the office, which happened to be where the only unlocked exit was, which we had worked out to be so as the prize prat that was Robbo, could make sure nobody snuck outside for a cheeky cigarette. Which only went to highlight another abuse of power from management in this shifty company, only managers could smoke in the office, which was unfair in my opinion, and I don't need to tell you what Jason thought of it.

'What the fuck do you losers think you're doing? Useless bunch of inept tossers!' continued Robbo, being his usual charming self, 'How fucking hard is it to get people, who want to buy property, to come and have a fucking look. You want a Ferrari like mine? Then pull your fingers out. We are one of the last, surviving property investment companies on this coast. Why? Because we push until we get results. So, everyone is staying another hour.'

It was the next action that changed my future, an action that wasn't started by me, I just happened to have made friends with a crazy, outspoken Australian.

'Fucking stress-head,' said Jason, looking at me and gesturing his head to the boss.

It didn't go unnoticed.

'What did you just say, shit head?' asked our fearless leader.

'Take it easy, Robbo, no-one's booking 'cause no-one's answering the phone,' explained Jason, quite reasonably I might add.

'What the fuck did you just say, little Australian cunt? You got something to say? How about you just walk out that fucking door?'

At this point, I had a decision to make. The problem is, with those split-second decisions, there's a good chance that the pressure of the situation doesn't help your mind compute and even when you try to do the right thing, it doesn't work out as one would have hoped.

Step in or stay out of it? That was the question.

'Steady on, Robbo. The footballs on at home, people aren't interested in talking to us while the game's on,' I said, in my most diplomatic voice.

'Shut your fucking mouth, Jimmy, you bald cunt,' was Robbo's reply.

I was stunned, speechless. I found his comment unfair; I shaved my head as I had thinning hair at this point, I wasn't bald exactly, just on the way. I don't mind saying that I was offended.

Jason, on the other hand, found Robbo's comment extremely funny.

'What?' I said, finally forcing out a word.

'You heard,' continued Robbo. 'If you've got a problem, there's the fucking door.'

I'd never been a fighter, but I wasn't a little boy any more, and accepting this kind of abuse on the phone was bad enough, but face to face bullying wasn't something I was going to accept.

Jason looked at me, and me at him, then we gathered our belongings from our desks and walked towards the exit. Every single one of the other telemarketers stood still, and in silence, afraid of losing their precious jobs, their gateway to financial security. Clearly they still believed the dream they had been sold during their two weeks training.

Robbo couldn't shut his mouth as we made our way to the exit.

'Fucking cowards. This was a chance for you to build for your futures, make more money than you could ever fucking dream of. You blew it, you couple of fucking losers,' he said, full of bravado in front of his remaining telephone slaves.

I could hear Jason muttering to himself under his breath.

As I opened the door, I turned to see Jason pick up a chair and move threateningly towards Robbo. I looked away and stepped outside, closing the door, being careful not to look through the window and see what happened.

I was a little partial to alcohol, and becoming slightly more dependent on Cocaine, but I've never been a violent person.

I didn't ask Jason if he hit Robbo with that chair, but one day he told me that he didn't, he stopped just before. He just wanted to scare him, show him that being the boss doesn't make you untouchable.

I think Jason has issues with authority.

7 – NO JOB. NO HOME?

I sat on the kerb by the road outside the office, head in hands and just a few feet from Robbo's prized possession, the red Ferrari. Jason came out and stood over me.

'What's up with you?' he asked, seemingly ignorant to the consequences of quitting a job.

'What's up with me? We've just lost our jobs, Jase. I'll have to leave the apartment,' I said, 'which leaves me stranded in Spain without a pot to piss in.'

I sighed, a deep sigh, the kind of sigh that signals a sense of realisation, of defeat, of helplessness. I looked up to see Jason, chin cupped in his hand, thoughts whirling around his mad, little mind.

His eyes widened, he'd had an idea. I braced myself.

'Don't worry about it. You're lucky I like you, Jimbo' he said. 'We got a spare room at our place. It ain't much, but it's gotta be better than sleeping on the beach.'

I didn't need long to think about the offer.

'Are you sure, Jase? Is it good to move in tonight? I don't fancy they'll want me staying in the staff digs anymore.'

'Yeah, right,' he continued, suddenly less convincing. 'First things first, we'll have to pop into

Sarah's bar on the beach front. We'll have to make sure she's alright with you staying. It should be cool, though.'

'Alright, sound. Then we can start thinking about finding some new jobs.'

We walked away from the office, but not after Jason spat out some phlegm onto the bonnet of Robbo's car.

'Petty,' I thought, but under the circumstances, acceptable.

It wasn't far to Sarah's bar. The office, that we'd never have the pleasure of slaving away in again, was right in the middle of the town, in a good building in a good location, surrounded by restaurants, bars and close to the beach. I reasoned now that this was to keep up the façade of living that dream that we'd been promised. Money, glamour, power, and all that other stuff you get with it, a bit like being on the set of one of those MTV videos.

'Don't worry about it, dude,' said Jason, 'there's loads of bar work around these parts, you'll be earning by tomorrow night easy.'

This 'caring', reassuring side of Jason made me nervous, it didn't suit him, it didn't come across as natural. I felt like the closer we got to Sarah's bar, the less positive he was about her allowing me to stay in her home. And although Jason was highly volatile, dangerous if you caught him at the wrong moment, I knew he saw me as a friend, and that he didn't want to let me down, or see me with no place to go.

'Bar work ain't exactly my thing, Jase,' I

replied, 'I'm meant to be here making something of myself, not pulling pints for pissed up holiday makers.'

'I've told you before, Jimbo, if you get work in the right bar, you can earn hundreds a week just in tips easy. Plus your basic. I mean it man, its sick!'

I could tell he was being honest here, or at least he really believed in what he was saying. But after hearing the bullshit that we'd heard over the last few weeks, my confidence in people and what they said on this coast had wavered enormously.

I was completely sober, and fully aware that at that moment in time, I was following a young, aggressive, drug taking, beer drinking Australian to his Cocaine-handling land-lady in hope of somewhere to stay. These were the people I was relying on? I was nervous.

'Yeah, we'll see. I'll take a look in the paper tomorrow. Maybe there's something else that'll suit, in an office or something,' I said, optimistically.

'It's your call mate, but I don't reckon you'll find much better than working for those pricks back there. And I don't think much of your sales technique either, if I'm honest.'

'You're probably right mate, you're probably right.'

Sarah sat in her cosy little wine-bar on the beach-front; comfy sofas and candles gave the place a warm feel, definitely decorated with a woman's sensual touch.

Adoringly, she admired the engagement ring on the hand of the female customer she was talking to. The woman's baby girl was sound asleep in a pram beside her.

'Well to be honest, if the baby hadn't have come along, who knows if her dad would have ever asked me to marry him?'

'You think it made him feel obliged to commit to you both?' asked Sarah, careful not to sound too intrusive. She was good at that; subtle manipulation.

'Not obliged, I hope! But I think it did give him a nudge in the right direction.'

'Well, she's beautiful. You're a very lucky woman.'

The woman's partner walked out of the toilet and towards the table where the girls were sitting.'

'Well, I'll leave you to it,' she said. 'Enjoy your wine.'

Sarah gets up and walks behind the bar, and looks back at the little girl asleep in her pram, then at the man who is now sat at the table seemingly happy and in love with his little family.

Even this far from the table, Sarah could still see the ring on the woman's finger, shining, sparkling. She wanted one, and she knew it.

'Hey, Sarah, how's it going?' asked Jason.

Sarah snapped out of her trance and saw her tenant and some stressed-out, bald guy dressed in a suit, me, the other side of the bar. I stood almost open-mouthed at how gorgeous this woman was. It was potent, in your face gorgeous. She ignored my blatant stare and checked her watch.

'You're finished early,' she said, 'let out for good behaviour?'

'Something like that, yeah. Listen, this is Jimbo. You got a minute?'

'What do you want this time, Jason?'

'Just a quick word,' he said, then he flashed that smile he uses like there's no tomorrow.

It softened her up, impressively, like it did with a lot of women. 'Lucky bastard' I thought, my only defining talent is a receding hairline, and none of the women I'd met were really digging that.

'Grab a table, I'll bring a couple of beers over if you'd like,' she said before turning to me, 'you do like beer, James?'

'James?' laughed Jason.

'Oh, and he prefers 'Jimbo' does he, Jason?'

She looked back at me, her beauty made me nervous.

'You can call me James, or Jimbo, Jimmy, anything.'

I felt like Hugh Grant, waffling away. What an idiot.

As me and Jason made our way to a table in the corner, Sarah reminded him that he wasn't at home, and beer in the bar wasn't free. She'd be adding these to his tab. It occurred to me that Jason had never brought me to Sarah's bar before, but clearly he drank there fairly often as he had a running tab.

'Yeah, yeah,' he called back to her. 'Just bring yourself with a couple of beers when you're ready.'

I sat down, facing the bar, and heard her say something under her breath. As far as I made out, she'd said 'Don't get cocky in front of your mate, Jason.' I wondered if these two were as good friends as Jason had led me to believe. In mind of the favour we were about to ask, I hoped they were.

'She's gorgeous, Jase,' I said.

Jason leant into the table and quietly told me to put my tongue back in my mouth, that I was likely to dribble all over her.

'And she's got a fella,' he explained, 'and believe me he's not one to cross, so keep your eyes and your hands to yourself.'

I tried to change the subject by gesturing towards the small candle that shone on our table, then I winked at him, but he ignored me.

'Anyway,' he continued, 'if you're moving in, the last thing I need is to be caught in the middle of that shit. I can see the papers now, jealous Moroccan boyfriend beats down girlfriends bit on the side, English dude thrown off balcony.'

I didn't think that any respectable newspaper would print a story using phrases such as 'beats down', 'bit on the side' or 'English dude', but I got his point. He didn't want to be caught in the middle of some complicated love affair, which seemed highly unlikely to me anyway. Sarah was hot, clearly had money and was seeing some drug-dealing bad-ass.

'I shouldn't think I'm her type,' I said.

'So what are you boys talking about,' asked Sarah, who appeared from nowhere over Jason's shoulder.

Jason looks up at her and gives her another smile.

'We're actually just discussing living arrangements,' he said.

'Ok.' She put down a beer each in front of us and continued, 'So what do you want to speak to me about?'

Jason shrugged his shoulders, maintaining eye contact with her as he said, 'the same thing really.'

'What do you mean, Jason?'

My mouth was dry, but I was too nervous to take a sip of the ice-cold beer that was just inches away from my fingers.

'Jimbo needs somewhere to live, and we have a spare room,' he said.

'And you thought you'd offer out my spare room?'

I felt a little awkward. I grabbed my beer and sunk a large gulp.

'Come on, Sarah,' he went on, 'it's a small room, with a bed, and we don't use it.'

'Listen, Sarah,' I cut in, much to Jason's annoyance going by the look on his face, 'I don't want to be a pain.'

She took a deep, almost measured breath, as if she was counting to ten in her head.

'How desperate are you?' she asked.

'He's desperate.'

Apparently it was Jason's turn to cut in, and he caught a glare from Sarah for his troubles.

'Can he not speak for himself?'

'You obviously haven't heard him on the phones at MacArthur's,' he said.

The joke at the expense of my failed sales career went over Sarah's head. She looked back to me.

'Yes, I can,' I said, with surprising confidence. 'Look, Sarah, I walked out of my job today, and that means giving up my digs. I'm quiet and tidy; you won't even notice I'm there.'

'So, if you have no job, how are you going to pay the rent? This is my apartment, not a doss-house for bums.'

'I've got money, enough to last a few months, at least. And I'll find another job. I'll start looking tomorrow.'

Sarah eyed me up and down, I wondered what she thought of me, was the underweight, balding, jobless, young man her type? She raised her hands and pointed her beautifully manicured hands at us both.

'Ok. But, any fucking about from one of you, and your both out, understand?'

'That's cool,' I said.

'Alright, rock on,' said Jason, picking up his beer and necking half of it in one go. He pulled out a five euro note from his pocket and pushed it into Sarah's hand.

'Put that towards my tab,' he said, knowing full well that it wouldn't even cover the beers we were currently drinking.

'Enjoy your drink, James. And Jason, can I have a word please?'

Sarah made her way behind the bar and Jason moved up to it and sat on a stool opposite her. I knew they'd be talking about me, but had faith, for some reason, that Sarah was a woman of her word. She'd let Jason live with her, and now me when I needed it, she was nice, I had no reason to doubt that.

'You put me on the spot then, Jason,' said Sarah.

'Yeah, I'm sorry, I didn't really think.'

'So what's he like?'

'He's cool, Sarah, I swear.'

'How do you know? How do you know he isn't a thief or a pervert? Or some of the other scum you get around here?' she asked, of which I heard most of.

'Look, he backed me up today at work, stood up to that dick of a boss, Robbo, when nobody else would even look him in the eye. He's safe, Sarah, I'm telling you.'

Sarah had just learnt a new piece of information.

'What happened with your boss? Have you walked out as well?'

'Yeah, I had to. He was talking all sorts of shit, calling us worthless, stupid, fucking this and fucking that. I had to walk,' he explained, as if we had no choice or sway on how things panned out back at the office. 'Anyway, you said you'd call your man at the Trikki Beach Club about that bar job.'

'You push your luck sometimes, Jason.'

'I know,' which he did, 'but this is the last time I promise.'

Sarah shook her head.

I sat watching her body language, and saw clearly that her tolerance of Jason was wearing thin.

'I'll call him later and let you know,' she told him. 'Now go and get James settled at ours. I'll see you at home.'

She picked up a cloth and started wiping down the bar.

'You're a legend Sarah. I don't know what I'd do without you.'

She didn't look up. Jason took the hint and walked towards the door. I took this as my sign to leave, dropped ten euros on the table to cover the beer and followed him out.

8 – THE NEW ABODE

I'd hardly slept that first night in Sarah's apartment. Not due to Cocaine, for a change, as that always kept me awake long into the early hours. But I was worried. I sat up talking to Jason, 'shooting the shit', as he'd say, which meant general banter, though I wasn't much in the mood for jokes.

He searched the apartment for Cocaine at one point, but couldn't find any. It annoyed him that he wouldn't be getting high.

'I bet she's gone through it all herself,' he said, 'greedy cow.'

I'd thought briefly about going back to MacArthur Realty International and asking for another chance, but that idea didn't last long. I remembered how bad I was at the job, and how I much I hated it. It wasn't for me.

Fair play to those who can put themselves through that, on the off-chance that MRI is actually a reputable company who pays its employees the agreed commissions, as opposed to the rumours that Jason had heard and was drip-feeding to me; that it was just a huge, marketing machine of a scam. Apparently Mr MacArthur didn't pay half of what he owed to his staff, who sold the properties that may or may not even exist. Nice guy.

My lack of sleep didn't stop me getting up

bright and early, aided that is by the open window shutters and the sun blazing through the opening and nearly burning holes in my eyelids.

My room was small, just a bed, a bedside table and a small wardrobe, but it was fine for me. The apartment in general was ok and typical for this part of the world, from what I'd seen so far, anyway.

I'd been out in the morning to get more cigarettes and a newspaper, 'The Sur in English,' a local rag for the many English speaking ex-pats. I also bought a pair of cheap flip-flops, the first pair I'd owned in my life. I felt ridiculous walking in them, pasty white legs hanging out of my one pair of shorts, my Arsenal football shirt sticking to my back and chest, thanks to the sweat that escaped my overheating body through every pore.

I managed less than fifteen minutes, sitting on a bench, trying to enjoy the sun before retreating back to the apartment, which I didn't find straight away. I really was lost at one point, but stumbled across the burnt-out moped opposite the apartment block that I'd noticed earlier on.

Jason wasn't there when I got back, and the door to Sarah's bedroom was still closed, so I didn't know if she was still in bed or had also gone out.

I filled a glass of water and took it, along with the paper into the front room, which wasn't home to much; a couple of sofas opposite each other, separated by a coffee table and vase, a sideboard with small television and an old looking drinks cabinet, and by the back wall was a larger table and chairs.

With difficulty, I peeled off my 2005/06

season claret football shirt, the one commemorating the time that the Gunners spent at Highbury, the shirt I love, and tossed it on the sofa.

I sipped my water and screwed my face up at the taste of it, that'd be why the fridge was half-full with water bottles, I realised. I scoured through the newspaper until I found the 'job opportunities' page. My heart sunk when I saw the lack of opportunities that there actually were.

Keen not to let my spirits down, I started to read the adverts from the top of the page, believing that someone, somewhere, would be looking for an eager member of staff, and had a job that would interest me, maybe even excite me, and give me a happy reason to get up each morning.

A couple of minutes into my search for a new future, Sarah walked into the front room, carrying a cup of coffee and wearing a bikini-top and pair of denim shorts. Even when wearing no make-up, she was beautiful. I took my bare feet off of the coffee table before she told me off on my first day in her home.

'Good morning, James,' she said, in a soft tone. 'How are you settling in?'

'God, she sounds so sexy,' I thought.

I folded the paper and put it onto the coffee table, next to the awful looking vase (probably a valuable antique or something, but what did I know?), and gave Sarah my full attention.

'Yeah, thanks again for letting me stay, Sarah.' I said, trying to remain calm and cool, 'It's a nice place. Must've cost a pretty penny?'

'It was my dad's. He passed away a few years ago.'

'I'm such a dick,' I thought.

'Sorry,' I said.

'That's ok. He had it coming I guess, messing around with some of the naughty people on this coast. It's through dad that I met Amine.'

'Amine?'

'My boyfriend,' she said, unintentionally reminding me how insignificant I was to her. 'Did Jason not mention him? I'm sure you'll meet him at some point.'

Sarah started piling some paperwork that was sprawled across the bigger table.

'Oh, yeah, is he some sort of gangster, or something?' I asked.

She smiled to herself.

'No, not really, he's involved with some people I wish he wasn't, but we don't talk too much about what he gets up to. I'd only worry.'

'Oh. Cool.'

She turned to me and rolled her eyes.

'This is the Costa del Sol, James. Everybody who comes here is up to something or running from someone. Which is it for you?'

'Christ,' I thought, 'she's some kind of mind-reader.'

'I'm just trying something different, Sarah. Maybe make some money whilst living in the sun.'

'Oh yeah? So how much money exactly?'

Now, I hate it when people talk about money, like the types I'd just been working for, and alongside at MRI. It makes me uncomfortable. I'm not really money motivated, but do feel that pressure that society puts onto people to be successful, the most accurate measure of which is, how much money you've got.

But then I don't know what motivates me, which didn't seem to be a good thing to say to someone you fancy when you're trying to look cool, ambitious, driven.

'I don't know, enough,' I said.

'Great answer, Jim. Nice one, Mr Smooth,' I thought.

'Enough? You mean enough to pay the rent? To buy a car? A house? A plane?'

Hands on her hips, she stood before me, clearly seeing right through me and the confident façade that I'd been putting on. I wondered if she felt sorry for me, or concern.

'Just enough to retire,' I said, sarcastically, trying to lighten the topic of conversation.

'Well, I've been here long enough to know, that to earn enough to retire, it won't be from a job you find in there,' she said, pointing at the newspaper as she sat down and sipped her drink.

I picked up the paper again and stared blankly at the ink that covered its pages, not taking in any information, just coming to terms with how quickly Sarah seemed to have sussed me out to be in a bit of a pickle. I'd heard that people often come and go through Marbella, like many coastal towns apparently. Not many last the distance. I guessed she'd seen these types before, and there was nothing at present that would show her I'm any different.

I felt her gaze on me and turned to see her big, brown eyes fixed on me.

'Do you know where Jason is?' I asked, feeling awkward in the silence that filled the room.

'He's gone to Trikki Beach. He's got an interview for a job.'

'Fucking hell, he doesn't waste any time does he?'

'My friend runs the place. He owed me a favour.'

'Friends in high places, that's got to be handy. He got anything else going?'

'Well it's not what you know, it's who you know,' she said as she stood. 'And sorry James, I had to beg him to give Jason a chance. Don't worry you'll find something, I'm sure.'

She was more confident than me, as she gave me a wink then headed back to the kitchen.

'I'm heading that way if you want to take a look at where Jason's working. It's a nice bar,' she called out from the other room.

'Yeah, maybe another time,' I said, 'I really want to get another job sorted. I fear sitting around doing nothing could become a bad habit.'

'Another one,' I thought.

She leant back in through the doorway.

'You only quit your job last night; one day enjoying your freedom will not be the end of you.'

'Thanks, anyway. But I want to get a job. I'll see you later, yeah?'

'Ok, suit yourself,' she said. 'And James, when I get back I better not find you've done a runner and my place is empty.'

'Not a chance, Sarah, I'm good as gold me.'

I watched her leave, and wondered if she could feel my eyes caressing every inch of her exposed skin as she walked away. Even after she had gone, I found myself staring into the void she had left for a minute or two before I snapped out of it.

I straightened the paper in my hands and restarted my search for employment.

9 – THE PROPOSITION

I woke up, startled, to see Jason leaning over me with his big, ugly mug in my face.

'Wakey, wakey, Jimbo.'

I could feel the damp from my sweat, sticking my back and legs to the sofa. Outside it was dark, I looked at my mobile phone and saw that it was gone ten in the evening, I'd been asleep for a few hours, and felt groggy as hell so closed my eyes again.

Jason picked up the newspaper from the floor beneath me and saw all the red circles and crossings out that I'd made on the jobs page. He tossed the paper onto the coffee table and clapped his hands twice by the side of my head.

'Wakey, wakey, Jimbo,' he repeated.

Disturbing my sleep was something that deeply distressed me, and I snapped a little at the annoying git who wouldn't let me rest.

'Leave it out, Jase, fucking hell.'

'I've had the best fucking day,' he said.

'Good for you,' I said, as sarcastically as I could be with my current lack of energy.

'Look at you, all tired and shit. How'd the job hunting go?'

'Shit.'

It took a few hours to get through the

vacancies on offer on the newspaper, and the outcome was wasted phone credit and a depressing outlook. I sat up on the sofa and gestured for Jason to sit down on the sofa opposite, partly so he could listen, but more so he'd get out of my personal space.

'Nobody wants me,' I continued, 'so it's either getting work behind a bar, or stepping on the next plane home, tail between my legs and all.'

Sometimes his bullish behaviour would get on my nerves, but then Jason always had this positive thing going on, I'd never seen him get down, angry, yes, but never down in the dumps. This could be due to his alcohol and drug consumption, but I believed it was down, at least in part, to his nature. Jason was a fighter, in every conceivable way.

'Turn that frown, upside down, Jimbo,' he said.

He was also a big child.

'What are you on about funny-man?' I asked, before sipping the water I'd left from earlier, forgetting how awful the cloudy liquid tasted.

'You shouldn't drink the tap water, mate,' he said.

I rubbed my eyes, trying hard to awaken fully.

'Listen, Jimbo, are you ready?' he continued, 'you remember when we had that chat in the bar the other night?'

'We've spent a few nights in different bars, Jase, probably the only thing I do well.'

'Ok, firstly, stop feeling sorry for yourself, you're a grown man, act like one.'

'Ouch.'

I gave him my attention.

'I just worked a shift at Trikki Beach Club, straight from the interview, I got the job, but you don't wanna hear about that. But hey, there are people down there, with more fucking money than they know what to do with.'

'Money' I thought, and took a deep breath and stretched out my arms and chest. 'Where's this conversation heading?'

'So what are you saying, Jase?' I asked, mustering up as much enthusiasm as I could.

Jason moved from the other sofa and sat down beside me, I could see the seriousness in his eyes.

'I'm saying five different people asked me for Charlie today,' he said, 'I had to say no, obviously because I was working, I had none on me. But that's not the point. These guys had to go down the beach and score off one of the Negros who sets himself up there selling handbags and DVDs and shit. Then they'd have to sneak it back in between their butt-cheeks or some shit like that.'

He had that huge grin slapped right across his face, and held out his hands, like he wanted high-fives or a round of applause. I wasn't quite on the same page at this point

'Yeah, that's nice, and what?' I asked.

He shook his head, let out a deep sigh.

'And what, have you ever actually been listening to me?' he asked.

Now in my defence, most of his ideas and views on the world and the people in it were bizarre if not downright ludicrous, he had no real conception of repercussions or responsibilities, but I decided to keep my thoughts to myself at this point.

'This is a prime opportunity to stake a claim on our own patch,' he declared.

'What patch?'

'Trikki Beach.'

'The place where you've just got the job you wanted? You want to start knocking out Trumpet over the counter? Is that what you're saying?' I asked, feeling less surprised after I'd said it than when the thought first ran through my head. This was Jason 'I don't give a flying fuck' Dorris sat beside me.

'I'm serious, Jimbo,' he said. And he was. I could hear it in his voice. The jovial attitude had gone, and I knew then that he was deadly serious about having a go at this.

Was it curiosity that got me, or the realisation that at this moment in time, I didn't have anything to lose? I knew that even entertaining the idea was not a clever thing to do, maybe the heat had got to me.

'So tell me,' I said, 'what are you thinking, Jase?'

'I'm glad you asked.'

Jason painted the scene for me; a classy beach club by day that becomes a night club in the evening. The guests all follow a strict dress code, and are typically affluent, no chavs, the prices at Trikki Beach see to that.

'Everyone who enters the club gets searched, that's why nobody has sole rights for dealing, it's too difficult to get enough gear through, and too risky. Today, security had police come and arrest two Moroccans who they caught carrying Coke.'

He told me that the dealers were held in a small room, out of the way, but that no harm had come to them. Trikki Beach was an exclusive establishment, it didn't want drug dealers ruining its reputation, but handing out physical punishment would do just as much harm to its reputation as anything. This wasn't a shady little club in a backstreet of Las Vegas, this was the Costa del Sol, where millionaires would come and throw their money around, and nobody wanted the threat of a good beating for a behaving a little badly, even if drugs were involved. The only option for Trikki Beach was to deal with things to the letter of the law, which was also a little scary to me; Spanish prison? No thanks.

'So everyone gets searched,' I said, 'how do we get the gear in?'

Jason grinned at me.

'You said "we",' he said, pointing and laughing. 'You want in, don't ya?'

'I'm just asking the question, mate. How do you get the gear in past security?'

'When I said everyone gets searched, I meant only the patrons, not the staff, not one of them got searched today.'

'And you know all this after working one day there?'

'I told you, Jimbo,' he continued, 'I've been looking to do this. I've been watching everybody today, all day long. Security stayed by the doors at the front and the back, all day and night, unless called over by the management.

'The bosses don't want the big spenders disturbed or feeling threatened by meat-heads, so they're kept pretty much out of sight. Management walk around the club mingling with the patrons, but wearing Trikki Beach suits, so they're visible. They just walk around to keep their eyes on things, but that's cool, as long as you got a drink in your hand you'll be fine.'

I wasn't as sold on the idea as Jason.

'Except I'd be approaching strangers and offering them Class A drugs.'

'No, you won't,' said Jason, reassuringly, almost. 'The patrons trust the bar-staff, we kiss arse all day keeping these people happy. When I get asked, I let them know that you're the man to see.'

'But I still got to make the exchange in the bar, someone could spot me.'

'But I take the money, they take a seat. I give you a signal for how many bags they've paid for. You just drop off the bags at their table, in a cigarette box or box of matches, whatever. It doesn't matter.'

'You'll take the money over the bar?' I asked, 'Won't your boss get a bit suspect when he sees you shoving money down your pants?'

'My till and my stock will balance at the end of every night. That's all that matters. And that's for me to worry about.'

I had no idea how it works behind a bar, so I couldn't argue with him on this point.

'And what sort of signals are you thinking of? And how do I know how many bags and who?'

'You keep an eye on me. One finger for one bag, two fingers for two. If I need to point out a customer then fine, if you have to ask me to be sure, ok, I guess, but try and stay on the ball and it shouldn't be a problem.'

I yawned. As exciting as this was for Jason, I really wasn't sold on the idea, and felt the need for a large glass of water then a long sleep in a proper bed; the sofa hadn't done my back any favours.

'And the money, how much money do you think we could make there, seriously?' I asked, an all important question when discussing any proposed business opportunity, legal or not.

'Well it wasn't that busy today, and four guys approached me, all drunk. I reckon on a busy day, bearing in mind we're coming into season, say ten bags a day, if people only took one each. I'll be working six nights a week, that's sixty bags a week.'

Did I say that I wasn't money motivated? Well I'm not, but these figures were impressive, even to me.

'And you wanna know what makes it even better?' he went on. 'Bags don't go for sixty down there, they go for eighty.'

I wonder if Jason saw my eyes light up, if he could sense that I was getting butterflies in my stomach at the thought of actually making some decent money for the first time in my life. But selling drugs wasn't something I'd been into, ever. I couldn't see how that cap would fit me.

I'm too soft, too nice, and too polite. Weren't the best drug dealers built like brick shit-houses and covered in tattoos which showed which gang they belonged to?

'And how we gonna get all this gear? By the

sounds of it, we're gonna be going through quite a bit. Who can supply that sort of amount? Is it really possible to do this?' I asked, hoping the logistical problems of such an endeavour would make this thing a no-go from the off, thus stopping me from having to take control and make a decision for myself.

'Amine,' he said.

'Amine?'

'Yeah, Amine, the one and only,' he clarified. 'He hates me, but that won't stop him wanting to take my money. I'm gonna phone him in the morning.'

'Hang on, Jase,' I said, wanting him to slow down, 'I haven't said that I'm in yet. I don't know about this. Just let me sleep on it, alright?'

I saw the excitement drain from Jason's face, and it was left with that angry, dangerous look he liked to sport.

'You sleep on it Jimbo, but I'm doing this, and if you don't wanna do it, I'll find someone else who will. I let you stay here for a fucking reason, you know?'

I stood up and carefully stepped around him and headed towards to the door to the bedroom. I'd forget the water for now, I just wanted to close myself in my room and lock the door, before I came face to face with the violent Jason that had briefly crossed my path before.

It wasn't right that, fearing who seemed to be my only friend on this coast. I needed to have a long, hard think as to what my plans were.

'You wanna earn money, I'm giving you a chance to do it,' he called out from behind me. 'You walk away from this, what you gonna do? You said yourself you'd be going home. I'll help you pack your bags if you want.'

I didn't like this side of Jason.

10 – SEEKING COUNSEL

Morning had arrived and I was strolling down the high street in Marbella, the sun was shining and I was wearing my favourite polo shirt and jeans and sun glasses, finishing off my outfit with my new flip-flops. I knew the footwear didn't go too well with my look. Typically I'd be wearing some 'classics' or maybe even a pair of shoes if the occasion called for it. But it was too hot for trainers, and I wish I had some smarter shorts to wear as well.

It hadn't escaped me that I was wearing pretty much my best clobber just to go to the cyber café, back home I would have felt super-cool in my outfit, but the way people dressed in Marbella made me feel a little inferior. I guess to dress well you need money, which is one of the many things that I'm lacking at present. All the men were dressed smartly, and the women, well, weren't wearing much at all, but you could see the class oozing off of them.

I wondered if I'd ever get to sample one of the local dishy women.

I'd been calling my mum every week, not at a specified time or day, but just maintaining contact enough to keep her happy. This was the first conversation we were about to have since I lost the job a couple of days ago, and so I was nervous, not that I was going to tell her that I was now unemployed, but because I was going to have to lie to her.

My mum had always been pretty relaxed with me, but if I was ever caught being dishonest, I wouldn't hear the end of it, and what made it worse is that she always knew when I wasn't telling the truth. I think women have a built in lie-detector that switches on when they become parents.

'Hola, teléfono, por favor,' I said to the grumpy man behind the counter, and gestured to the phone booth in the corner that I had always used. He nodded, not taking his beady little eyes off me as I made my way to the back of the shop. I closed the glass door behind me and sat down on the stool.

'Just calm down and be happy. She just wants to know that I'm happy,' I told myself.

I took a deep breath and picked up the phone, dialling quickly so I didn't have time to change my mind. The phone seemed to ring for an age before connecting.

'Hello, this is Charlotte,' said the voice.

'Hi, mum, it's me,' I said, rather pointlessly.

'Sorry, but nobody is home right now. Please leave a message after the beep.'

'Answer machine, good, finally a bit of luck,' I thought. I could leave a message and buy a bit of time before having to give the old dear the inevitable bad news that she must have been expecting.

Even I could lie to an answer machine.

'Hey mum, just saying hello and seeing how

you're getting on. It's all good out here. I'll try and call you again sometime soon alright? Speak soon mum, I love you.'

I hung up the phone and wiped the sweat from my ever expanding forehead, I wasn't sure if the sweat was due to the pressure of that last phone call of the relentless heat, even in the phone shop with its collection of fans blowing on high power. I had to open the glass door to my cubicle to let the air circulate a bit.

'What to do now?' I thought, 'I need some advice.'

Sadly, the two people I'd usually turn to for advice, outside of the family, were Lee and Scott, who both weren't answering their phones for whatever reason. This led me to make a decision, phone Tom and explain the situation to him, knowing he loves to gossip and the whole of Hertfordshire would know about my predicament by this time tomorrow, or call Dave, modern days equivalent of a court jester.

'Dave Kibble residence,' he said as he picked up the phone, knocking an ashtray over as he did so.

'Hey, Kipper, it's Jimmy. What's the crack?'

'Funny-man, how's it going? I'm just getting high, waiting for the game. It ain't the same without you here to roll up for me.'

'Yeah, I thought you'd be doing something like that. Listen Dave, I need some advice man.'

At which point he almost choked on the spliff he was smoking, I can only assume due to the shock of me needing his help.'

'Fucking hell, Jim, you asking me for advice?' I was right. He continued, 'what's the crack, things fucking up over there or what? You want me to come over and kick some heads in?'

'No, funny-man, calm yourself down. I just left my job that's all, it didn't work out, and it's turning out to be difficult finding something else.'

I heard him stubbing out his joint and arranging himself on his sofa, for a moment I wished I was there with him, getting high, watching football or playing the Xbox, and then I remembered that I couldn't stand it in the end, getting high and drunk to make it all seem bearable.

'So are you coming back then?' he asked.

'I don't wanna. I ain't been out here a month yet, people are gonna take the piss something rotten.'

'Yeah, that's a bummer. How come you quit? What you gonna do now? You're right about people taking the piss though mate, I'll be first in line, and you know it.'

'Yeah, thanks for that.'

'You want my advice? Just do whatever you wanna do, mate. Even if you're only over there another couple of months, it's better than coming home now and being ripped to shreds by us lot.'

His advice was straight from the heart at least.

'Oh yeah, by the way,' he continued,' I saw Colleen last night with her new man, introducing him to people down the pub. He's a knob.'

I wish he hadn't told me. I didn't want to hear about Colleen and her new fella, out and about, probably hands all over each other and kissing and laughing and living happily ever after.

'Dave, I gotta go mate. Thanks funny-man.'

'Alright funny-man, you keep in touch yeah?'

'No worries. And Dave, do me a favour, don't tell anyone I've quit my job, I don't want the old dear finding out, she'll only worry.'

'No problem, my lips are sealed. And Jimmy, if you can't be good, be careful.'

All things considered, that was best advice he could have given. I put my finger on the button to end the connection, and then dialled a Spanish mobile number.

Jason was collecting glasses from tables by the restaurant part of the bar when his phone vibrated within his pocket. He looked around for management before answering the call.

'Hola,' he said, his Spanish was about as good as mine.

'Jason, it's me.'

'Jimbo.'

'What we talked about last night, count me in.'

I could hear that wide grin appearing on Jason's face from the other end of the phone, his cheeks pulling apart, exposing his pearly gnashers.

'You know it makes sense, mate. I knew you wouldn't let me down,' he said, back to friendly Jason in an instant.

'So what's the crack? What happens now?'

'I'll go to the bank on the way home to get my cash. We need four hundred euros each.'

'Four hundred Euros' I repeated.

'Yeah, eight hundred will get us twenty grams,' he explained. 'I'll call Amine and see if he can drop it off later. We might have to go and meet him though.'

'Alright, sound. I'll go to the bank now and get my cash out. What about scales?' I asked, giving the impression that I had a clue about being a good drug dealer.

'Already got some sitting in my wardrobe. I've had 'em ages.'

'Shit, you have been thinking about this for a while.'

'You know it, bro. Shit, I gotta go. I think the boss is giving me the eye.'

'Right, I'll see you at home.'

'Laters.'

I knew that what I'd just agreed to do was not a great decision, and tried to convince myself that at least a bad decision was better than not making a decision at all. But what I guess it came down to, was that I didn't want to go home to England, not yet, not back to that same routine. I wasn't ready, I hadn't got a clear picture of what I wanted from life, what I wanted to do with my days, so until that became clear, I was gonna go with the flow.

11 – INITIAL INVESTMENT

I was nervous again.

Since coming to Spain and moving out of my comfort zone, I had discovered that I am not a people person, I do not like change, and in fact, I very much like my comfort zone. There is good reason why it is called a comfort zone.

I had met more new people in the previous few weeks than ever before. Maybe not like when you first go to a new school but when you do that, you're always surrounded by a good number of your old school friends. Marbella wasn't like that.

First at MRI, being thrown into a job that wasn't anywhere near natural to me, working for venomous snakes in suits and being one of many anonymous nobodies who were being barked at all day, that didn't do anything to calm my nerves, or help me settle into my new lifestyle.

And then, even worse, I was alone in my new 'home', however temporary it was going to be, waiting for my psychopathic flat-mate, our over-the-top sexy landlady and according to Jason, 'Mr Dangerous' himself, Amine 'I'm a big, nasty, drug-dealing motherfucker' Arab guy, to come and do some Hollywood style drug deal.

Like I said, I was nervous.

I was praying that Jason would get home

before the other two, as he said he would on the phone, but you can't always believe what a Cocaine-sniffing nutter says to you, even if his heart is in the right place.

Interesting fact: Often, when you buy Cocaine, on a personal level, not to redistribute, necessarily, you get the shits. I mean that the thought, the excitement, of nearly having that first line, always the best of the night, was close again. Sometimes you can hold it in until after you've done that first line, other times, you have to use the toilet as soon as your dealer puts that wrap or bag of Charlie in your hand.

I was already so nervous that I manoeuvred to the bathroom, lowered myself onto the toilet seat, and let go of the cheap baguette that I'd eaten earlier, before it had fully formed and compacted itself ready for despatch, sweat gathered on my brow as I sprayed the back of the bowl. I heard the front door open and had to gather my wits, clean me and the toilet and open the window to allow in some fresh air within the space of seconds.

'Alright, bro?' asked Jason as I walked into the front room, 'You sure you're up for this?'

'No, Jase, I've been shitting my pants all day, I wanna go home, I need my mum, I don't wanna see you or your fucked up friends ever again.'

'Yeah? I thought so.'

He checked his watch, and pulled out his four hundred euros from his pocket.

'Good,' he said, 'they'll be any here any minute I reckon. You got the wedge?'

I pulled out my half of the money, which I had

arranged neatly in order of denomination, with the notes all facing the same way and the right way up, and gave it to him. He put all the money together, but not before I noticed Jason hadn't arranged his notes in orderly fashion at all.

'Messy bastard.'

'Listen, just be quiet when he gets here, he's quite funny with people he doesn't know, ok?'

'Great. You sure you don't want me to hide in the bedroom?' I said, half-serious.

'No, you stay here, just shut your mouth. This could be the start of something big, let's not rock the boat.'

The front door opened, and I heard Sarah's voice. Jason gestured for me to sit down, and then he sat beside me.

In walked the beautiful Sarah, followed by Amine, who was a tall, muscular Moroccan. First impressions were that he looked like he could handle himself, but nothing special. You'd see bigger and meaner looking men on the doors of most bars or clubs.

Sarah and Amine sat down opposite us on the other sofa, he stared at me, and I nervously tried to give him a wink, to show that I was a bit of a geezer, but he ignored me, which was predictable.

'I hear you're going into drug dealing, I take it there aren't many jobs out there at the moment?' said Sarah.

Jason and Amine looked at me. Shit, Sarah was talking to me.

'Yeah, Sarah, it seems that way.'

'Amine,' Jason piped up, 'this is Jimmy, and he's my partner.'

Amine put his arm around Sarah and pulled her close. I would say it was more an indication of possessiveness than affection, but I chose not to start that conversation.

'So you're the new bum she has taken in off the street,' he said, factually, staring right at me again.

'Yeah,' I said, 'something like that.'

'Something like that?' he continued, 'I'd say exactly like that.'

For a Moroccan living in Spain, he spoke good English. He had a very strong accent, but certainly knew how to make someone uncomfortable with a few choice words. 'Well done,' I thought, 'good show.'

Sarah slapped him on the thigh, and then he gave her a stern look.

'Leave him alone,' she said. 'Sorry, James, Amine doesn't do politeness.'

'That's fine, I can see his point,' I said, trying like hell not to look too fazed by the awful vibe in the room.

'Jason,' said the northern African, 'you have got some money for me?'

Jason took out the eight hundred euros and handed it over to Amine, it wasn't the moment to point out that the tidy four hundred of the eight hundred was from me, and the screwed up notes in no particular order were from my new business associate.

Amine didn't even look at the money to be honest, he just stuck it into an inside pocket of his jacket, then reached into another pocket and pulled out a cigarette box and tossed it over to Jason.

I watched as Jason opened the box, half expecting it to be empty and Amine to say 'you want your money back, come and get it.' But it wasn't empty, and Jason pulled out a plastic bag with about four or five Oxo cubes worth of Cocaine.

It was beautiful.

'That's twenty. There's plenty more where that came from. If you start buying in proper amounts I sort you out a better discount,' said Amine, and then he turned to Sarah, 'Come on, let's leave these two gays to it.'

'Leave 'em alone, you bully,' said Sarah, fully appreciating Amine's shit sense of humour. They stood and she led him to her bedroom, closed the door, and that was that.

'To be honest,' I said to Jason, 'that went better than I was expecting.'

Jason ignored me at first, he had other things on his mind, obviously the Coke, but then he turned to me and spoke in a low, confident whisper.

'I'll get him one day,' he said, but then perked up and continued with, 'for now though, let's try this shit out. You want a beer?'

He lobbed the bag of Charlie at me and made his way to the kitchen. I opened up the bag and the smell hit me straight away, that diesel kind of smell that I'd had make its way up my nostrils hundreds of times before. I tipped the bag up to get a couple of lines worth out and on the coffee table, but around a full gram tumbled out in rocky lumps, much more than we needed just for a taster.

'Oh, well.'

As I started hacking away at some of the

smaller lumps with my bank card, Jason came back into the room and put some beers on the table. I looked up to say 'cheers' and accidently caught the ugly vase with my elbow, nearly toppling it over.

'Jesus, man, careful, she loves that vase,' said the Aussie, as he disappeared back out of the door.

'Doubt it,' I thought, 'it's fucking hideous.'

Jason was back in an instant and put a fresh deck of cigarettes on the table with a clean ashtray and a drinking straw cut into two halves. He gave one to me and we both leant over the two giant lines I had prepared on the table.

We looked up at each other and smiled.

'You wanna go first?' I asked.

He thought about it for a moment, like there was something on his mind.

'No, mate, you go first. I gotta go take a dump.'

I didn't wait for a second invitation. I snorted that fat line of Cocaine up my nose in one go, it hit me so hard I thought my eyeballs would pop out. I lit up a cigarette and melted into the back of the sofa.

'I, absolutely, fucking, love, Cocaine.'

Jason had brought all the equipment to weigh up and bag the gear. We'd had a couple of lines each by now, and a couple of beers, and cigarettes, and we were ready to start the production line. We toyed briefly with the idea of cutting the gear, making it go further, but thought quality over quantity would be the better option, considering our potential client base at Trikki Beach. We were taking it all very seriously.

Back home in England, I'd normally receive my Powder in a wrap, folded paper making an envelope, or a bag, like a collectors bag that closed at the top when you squeezed it. In Spain, it was normal to get your gear inside little balls of plastic, sealed at the top by twisting it shut then burning it so the plastic kind of welds all the edges together, therefore sealing it completely.

It's a pain in the arse, to be honest, but apparently the heat in these parts makes the Cocaine melt into the paper and you lose your drugs. Nobody explained why you couldn't get it in the normal bags though; I guessed they just weren't available around here. Even the bag we got from Amine was a sandwich bag, and wasn't sealed shut when we got it, it was just tied off at the top in a knot.

So Jason would weigh up the grams, which were actually 0.8 grams, and place them on the small circles that I'd cut out of a plastic shopping bag. I'd then fold the edges up, hold the Cocaine in the make-shift bag between my fingers and twist the remaining plastic into a tail, which I would then burn to fuse the edges together and hey presto, I'd be left holding a little sack of Cocaine, ready for sale.

The problem for me was, burning and twisting the plastic was really bloody painful, I had blisters appearing on my fingers and we weren't even half way through the production run.

Jason noticed my pain and laughed, before standing up and going to the kitchen.

'You want another drink?' he asked.

'Yeah,' I said, finger and thumb in mouth, in an effort to cool them down.

He came back into the room and put a glass of whiskey in front of me.

'We're out of beer then?' I asked.

'That'll help you sleep mate,' he said. 'We got a long night tomorrow night.'

He took a sip from his own whiskey and dropped onto the table some sandwich bag plastic ties.

'Use them if you want,' he said, helpfully, 'they'll be easier on your fingers, you big girl.'

'You mean to say we could use these instead of sticking my fingers on burning plastic?'

'Well, it's got to be easier right? Pass me the scales. Drink your drink.'

I sipped my awful tasting whiskey and sparked another cigarette whilst Jason took it upon himself to rack up another couple of lines.

'Just another little one to keep us going,' he said.

There was no argument from me, as I've said before, stopping after that first one is almost impossible, especially when you're surrounded by loads of little piles of it.

'And I forgot to say, Jimbo, from tomorrow I'll be working late shifts, indefinitely.'

I asked myself if this affected me in any way, and I realised that my working hours would also change. Not that it mattered, having the day to myself and working at night was probably a good thing, benefit from the sunshine and stuff.

'We'd probably sell more at night anyway,

don't you think?'

'Yes, Jimbo, that's why I asked for the shift change,' he replied 'Business is gonna boom.'

By the time I got to bed it was nearing four o'clock in the morning. It always amazed me how, when high, I would lose concept of time. One minute we were bagging up drugs and drinking and smoking, and the next, we'd run out of cigarettes, so we decided to call it a night.

I was lying on my bed, hot and restless. The whiskey didn't help send me to sleep after all. But I kind of knew that would be the case, I always had trouble sleeping after a few lines, even one line keeps me awake for longer than I'd like.

I realised that I hadn't eaten for hours and hours, and although I felt a little empty in the stomach, I didn't really have an appetite. Again, this was normal for me when abusing The White Stuff.

My nose was constantly running, which was a reaction of my membranes to the Cocaine, or the stuff they use to make the Cocaine, depending on who you asked, and I was constantly rubbing my nostrils and top lip with a tissue; I could feel my face getting sorer at every wipe.

I also had a choice to make concerning the window, do I close it and sweat like a pig, or leave it open and risk a mosquito sniffing me out and coming to pester me? Neither of the two options would be that serious if I could sleep, but being awake and going through either of them was a real head-fuck. I left the window and took my chances with the mosquito, which never showed. In fact, it was the sound of birds singing that disturbed me, when it began to get light, and then it was morning.

The news that we'd be 'working' the late shift sounded even more appealing to me at this point. I closed the window and the shutter and would just have to deal with the heat. It was time to sleep, my body and my brain were ready to shut down.

I don't know what time, but eventually I drifted off, thoughts of my mum, the people sleeping in the apartment that I hardly knew, and also of the plan for tomorrow night running through my head. Also, I thought, even without the Cocaine, I'd have enough to give me sleepless nights.

12 - SHOWTIME

Jason took the gear to the club as planned. I arrived later, met him in the toilets and took the product. After last night we were left with twenty-two bags weighing in at 0.8 grams.

I set up camp in a corner near Jason's bar and made a drop-off whenever he gave me the signal. The fact I needed a drink in my hand to not look out of place meant I was quickly getting more and more pissed, other than that, things were going alright.

And being a little drunk had its upside, I was feeling a lot more relaxed than I was on the way here in the taxi, but then it also had its downside, I'd swaggered into a couple of girls earlier, fortunately none of the security or management staff saw as I'm sure that have something to say, but Jason saw, and I saw the look on his face, which wasn't happy.

When I'd finished another bottle of beer, I went to the bar to ask Jason for a fresh one.

'Maybe you need to slow down mate, you're looking a little worse for wear,' he said, actually meaning, 'stop drinking, you're fucking drunk and making me angry.'

I grabbed onto the side of the bar as I felt my legs wobble beneath me, 'maybe he's right,' I thought.

'Open one of the bags and rack up a little one,' he said, 'It'll wake you up a bit. And then let me know how many are left.'

'Yes, boss,' I said, maybe a little too sarcastically.

'Fucking English,' I heard him say under his breath.

Ignoring his remark, I composed myself and slowly made my way to the men's room, doing my best to avoid the men and women who flirted and danced and all the other stuff that people with social skills do when they are out and about.

I locked myself into a cubicle and counted the bags out onto the closed toilet lid, there were ten left. I took out my bank card and untied one of the bags, stuck the corner of the card inside and as carefully as I could in the state I was in, lifted out a little heap of Coke and brought it up to my left nostril; my preferred 'snorting nostril'. With my other hand I pushed my right nostril closed and inhaled sharply through the nose, sucking up the Powder so hard and fast that it could have passed through the inside of my nose and crashed into my brain.

Then I did one more for luck.

Within seconds, I could feel a slight grin pulling across my face, and a bowel movement ready to go in my stomach. I gathered up the remaining bags of Trumpet, bagged them and stuck them in my pocket; put my card away and then dropped my guts all over the nice, clean toilet bowl.

Trousers and pants around my ankles, I sat back and closed my eyes, took a deep breath, and enjoyed the chemical reaction that occurred in my body as the Cocaine did what it does best.

I was no longer drunk, I was high and drunk; not perfect, but a definite improvement.

I slapped cold water on my face after I washed my hands and stared into my reflection in the mirror.

'Sort yourself out, Jimmy.'

The lack of sleep from the night before had left its mark on my face. I had bags under my eyes and was paler than usual, so I reminded myself that the Cocaine wasn't going to be a regular thing. From now on, I would only use it if like tonight it was a better idea than not using it.

In hindsight, my logic was fucking ridiculous and deeply flawed, but that's a druggie for you.

I walked back through the bar, confidence restored and my spirits lifted. I asked Jason for a bottle of water, which he dutifully slammed down in front of me.

'That's three euros for the water,' he said. 'And there's a fat guy in a red shirt at the table behind you, three's his favourite number. How many we got left?'

I counted out three euros in change and stacked them gently in front of Jason.

'Six, after these three are gone. And I got one open in my wallet.'

'Cool. Are you good to carry on? Or you too pissed?'

'I'm good. I'll be at my table,' I answered.

I grabbed another couple of boxes of 'gratis' Trikki Beach matches from the bar and took my bottle of water over to the small table that I'd claimed earlier.

I took a sip of drink before opening a box and tipping the matches out into my hand; I stuck them into my back pocket and left the box open on the table. I then shoved a hand into my pocket and counted out three bags of Powder, and then lifted them discreetly up under the table, and brought down the empty box and stuffed it full of the drugs. Sounds simple? Not really when you can't look at what you're doing as you have to keep an eye out for anyone who is taking too much notice. Luckily, the bar was busy, and nobody really took notice of the man stood in the corner drinking on his own.

And then I did what I'd been doing all night.

I went to the table as instructed by the Aussie, put an arm around the shoulder of the fat guy in the red shirt and slipped the matchbox into his hand.

'The barman said you left these at the bar,' I had taken to saying, which hadn't overly-confused anybody as of yet.

And then I slipped away.

Sometimes the buyers would offer a drink, or want a chat, but more often than not, they would head straight to the toilets to either check the merchandise or get high, probably both.

The next couple of hours went fast. I sank one more beer and another bottle of water, smoked far too many cigarettes and also finished off the bag of Trumpet that I'd opened earlier.

I was fucking steaming.

With regards to our enterprise, I'd made three more drop-offs, leaving just two bags in my pocket.

I could feel my jaw muscles clenching

together, and I was grinding my teeth. I could only imagine what I must have looked like, so I went over to the bar and waited until I got Jason's attention, having to turn away two other barmen as I stood there. Jason finally approached and I leant in towards him so I didn't have to shout.

'Jase,' I said, 'I gotta go. I'm tripping my nuts off.'

'There's two left?' he asked, looking around the bar to see where his colleagues and bosses were. They were too close I assumed, as he had a look of disappointment on his face. He wanted some gear, but couldn't risk being seen exchanging little packets of anything at the bar.

'Save me a bag,' he continued, 'leave it in my room.'

'No problem,' I said, turning away.

'Jimbo.' he called out.

I turned back, and he gestured for me to lean in again.

'Don't do all the gear,' he said, clearly believing that I could go through the last two bags on my own at home.

As it happens, he was half right, I went through one of them, and I didn't really sleep, maybe a couple of hours, on and off. That made two nights on the bounce, not clever.

13 - PAYDAY

I heard Jason moving about in his bedroom, threw on some jeans and grabbed a polo shirt and socks then went to see what he was up to.

I stuck my head through the door and saw he was sat on his bed in just his work trousers and had just snorted a line of Coke. He put the CD case with the traces of Powder onto his bedside table and adjusted his position before waving me in.

I put my shirt on first, as two men, topless in a bedroom at the same time made me feel uncomfortable. I sat at the bottom of his bed and pulled my socks on.

'You found the gear alright then,' I said, nodding to the open bag of Trumpet next to the straw, bank card and CD case.

It was then that three piles of money next to the drug paraphernalia caught my eye. He picked one up and passed it to me, I didn't know off-hand how much was there, but it looked like a fair amount, and it felt good to hold.

'This is mine,' he said, dropping another pile of paper into the drawer of his table, 'and this is for Amine,' he said, as he picked up the last pile, folded it and placed it into a packet of cigarettes, taking out the last cigarette as he did so.

'Not bad for a night's work,' I said, as I

counted out three hundred and sixty euros in crumpled up bank notes, straightening them out and putting them in order.

'Pretty good, mate,' said Jason, 'but you can't get that drunk when you're carrying this Shit, Jimbo, you gotta keep your wits about you.'

He decided not to smoke the cigarette and tossed it into the same drawer where the money was, then adjusted himself on the bed, stretching out and almost catching me with his feet as he did so.

'And listen, I gotta get some sleep,' he continued, 'so you'll have to meet Amine later on. He's got your number. He'll call you later this afternoon and meet you in town.'

'Great. The man hates me, Jase.'

'He hates everybody,' he replied, 'but I reckon we got a good thing going 'ere, so just meet him, give him the cash and take the Powder. Easy.'

'Right,' I said, unconvinced.

'And it's gonna be tight for time later, I gotta be at work by eight,' he went on, 'so you'll have to get back here so we can bag up the gear as soon as you've seen the big man.'

I noticed that when Jason talked of Amine, when Cocaine was the subject of conversation, that he held a tone of respect in his voice, unlike when Amine was mentioned in relation to Sarah, when it was quite the contrary.

'No problem,' I said. 'I'll come back straight away. I don't fancy hanging about the town with twenty in my pocket, anyway.'

I noticed Jason was almost asleep, almost straight away after sniffing a line. Maybe he'd had one of his glasses of whiskey to help him relax. Whatever it was, I wish I had that kind of control over my body, instead of lying there, wide awake into the night, not being able to switch my mind off.

I picked up the cigarette carton and remembered about the wedge of cash I had just received. Closing Jason's bedroom door behind me, knowing that I had the displeasure of meeting Amine later on, I thought I'd treat myself to a bit of shopping, maybe a proper meal.

Maybe with some new clothes and some decent food inside of me, I wouldn't feel so out of place in this millionaire's playground.

I'd always liked a good watch, not that I'd ever had one. The nicest watch I'd ever had was a gift from Colleen, my ex, but even that wasn't as classy as I might have liked.

I stood looking through the window at the different watches on offer. You could buy any old watch from as little as forty euros, but if you had more money than sense, you could easily pay up to ten thousand euros on a small piece of wrist-wear that indicated what the time was. And they were just the timepieces on display in the window, who knew what they've got stored behind the counter and under higher security inside the jeweller's?

Maybe it was the lack of a decent night's sleep, or perhaps it was a delayed fear of the police in relation to my new occupation, but the gentle tap I felt on my shoulder made me jump out of my skin.

'Sorry,' said the friendly, familiar voice, 'did I

scare you, James?'

'Sarah,' I said, relieved to turn and see the gleaming smile of Sarah before me.

'Are you buying me a ring already?' she asked, I could have sworn flirtatiously. 'We've only just met.'

'That's very funny, Sarah. Actually, I was looking for a watch.'

'Well, then let me help you,' she said, leaning closer to the window, and closer to me at the same time. I could smell the fresh, cleanliness of her. I just wanted bury my head into her neck, taste her skin, breathe her scent.

'Be my guest,' I said, having to pull my eyes away from her and back to the watches that I'd all but forgotten about in just an instant.

She put her arm around my shoulders and directed me to the items behind the glass, giving me her opinions as she dragged me slowly from one side of the shop-front to the other.

'Never buy a plastic or Velcro sports-watch, you are not a child,' she said. 'Do not buy a digital, unless you are stupid. Diamonds, these are a girl's best friend, remember that for when you buy me a watch.'

'Is she flirting with me? Or is she just like this with everyone?'

I hoped to God that she didn't notice the movement at the front of my jeans, the sound of her voice, almost whisper-like but so strong in my ears, sending tingles down my spine and hot pulses to my manhood.

'Men shouldn't be too flashy,' she said. 'Maybe get a watch that reflects your personality?'

She stopped and pointed to a silver watch through the window. It wasn't much to look at, but clearly well-made and solid looking.

'Are you calling me simple?' I asked.

'No, James. I believe you're the strong, silent type.'

I felt like I was falling in love.

Then she took her arm from my shoulders, turned and left, leaving me stood by the window, but watching her not the watches, as she walked away, taking my breath away with her.

I finally lost sight of her. She had disappeared amongst the crowd of people out on this sunny morning, so turned my attention back to the watch she had pointed out to me. I wondered how much damage Sarah could do to men's wallets if she was an actual saleswoman, I imagine a lot.

I'd received the call from Amine, which was an awfully difficult conversation over the phone, which led me to believe he was stoned, or that his English didn't convey itself very well unless spoken in person with someone.

Regardless, I was now stood at the back of a car park near the town centre, wearing my new watch and carrying an Armani shopping bag, which held a very expensive piece of cloth that disguised itself as a short-sleeved shirt. For a moment, I felt guilty about spending so much money on one piece of clothing, but then I remembered how I had made the money in the first place, and thought my guilt to be a little misplaced.

'Fuck it,' I thought.

A beaten up, old BMW pulls into the car park and heads in my direction. The music, maybe Moroccan or Tunisian or something like that, turned down as it drew closer. I saw Amine wasn't alone. There were two others with him, also of North African appearance. The car stopped beside me and Amine hardly acknowledged me as he spat out of the window onto the floor, not too far from my feet.

'Have you been waiting long, Jimmy?' asked Amine, still not looking at me.

'Half hour,' I said, whereas in fact it was nearer an hour, I just didn't want him to know that, or the fact I was worried about him wanting to rip me off, which only heightened when I saw that he'd come with 'reinforcements.'

He turned towards his buddies in the car, said something in Arabic and they all laughed.

I didn't know if Amine was as hard or as dangerous as Jason had always made out. But he was a bully. And a prize cock, too, if I'm to be honest. He wasn't the first idiot I'd met in my life, and surely wouldn't be the last. I don't pretend to be a hard man, but I really can't stand to be bullied, it makes my blood boil.

Smiling, he turned back to me, and for the first time made real eye contact.

'You got the money?' he asked.

I pulled out the cigarette packet from my pocket and tossed it into the car, it landed in his lap. Without checking the carton, he opened the glovebox and threw it in, pulling out a different box, which he then chucked out of the window. It landed on the floor, right next to his spit.

'You might want to take better care of that, Jimmy,' he said, as he turned up the volume on the car stereo, put the car into gear and slowly pulled away.

I watched the car circle the car park and head to the exit, then out of my line of sight before I bent over and picked up the package he had thrown at my feet.

I opened the box and gave a sigh of relief to find the Trumpet inside. I closed it up again, dropped it into my carrier bag and headed home.

14 – TIME GOES BY

The next few months went well, on the business front at least.

We were now shifting the best part of thirty bags a night, six nights a week, so the money was rolling in. We were buying in fifty grams at a time, not for any cheaper as Amine had originally said, but we still made a healthy profit, with the added benefit of not having to meet Amine as often to score the drugs, so I didn't mind.

On the down side, the more time I spent in the club, the more Cocaine I went through. I couldn't remember the last time I'd eaten more than one decent meal in a day. I'd get the occasional night sleep, if that's what you'd call it, more likely it was my body saying 'no more', and turning itself off for seven hours or so.

Speaking of my body, I'd lost over a stone in weight since arriving in Spain, and I was never the biggest guy in the first place. Clothes that I'd bought when the first lot of drug money started to come were now too big for me, hanging off my shoulders in like a school-kid being forced to wear his older brother's hand-me-downs.

On top of that, I was having problems with my nose. Not quite the problems that the papers had so keenly reported about Danniella Westbrook, detailing how her nose had collapsed completely, but I worried I was on the way there.

I was having nose-bleeds every day or so, just a little bit of blood, but even when it wasn't bleeding, I constantly had to wipe it or blow it. It was a real pain in the, well, in the nose.

I'd even taken to the habit of using my right nostril, which just didn't feel right. It was like wanking with the wrong hand. And after a couple of lines and a beer or two I'd forget about the change of technique and revert to my preferred way.

There was no way to deny it; the Cocaine had well and truly sucked me in.

I knew I was worse than ever before, like I knew that it wasn't clever and that wasn't what I really wanted, but the habit was there, it had clawed its way into my daily routine and I couldn't shake it.

It was like I needed a jolt of some sort, fuck, I would have taken an electric shock to the head if I thought it would help.

When Jason didn't work, he liked to enjoy his evenings with a bit of the Powder and lots of the booze. Then one night, he'd thought of something special to do, 'a surprise' he said, he was bored of Marbella and Puerto Banus, the little party port along the road, and as always, I went along with it rather than argue with the mad-man.

So we sniffed drugs in the back of a taxi during the twenty minute journey out of Marbella, and ended up in Club 92, a bar which also doubled up as a brothel.

'I can't believe it, dude,' said Jason, wide-eyed and as happy as a pig in shit, 'Look around, man. This is fucking awesome, bro.'

Other than when he was counting his money, this was the happiest I'd seen Jason for a while. Things seemed to be getting a little stressed between him and Sarah recently, so I was happy for him, even if I did feel like a fish out of water.

The bar was crowded with stunning young women, eastern European looking and sounding, wearing provocative underwear and strolling around the place offering their services. I hadn't yet been cornered by one of them, and Jason could see how nervous I was.

What I should tell you, is that when you have a pretty bad drug habit, like taking Cocaine every day; the drug-high can actually become the highest priority, more so than sex. At this point in my life, I preferred shoving Powder up my nose, than putting my penis into gorgeous-looking women for nothing other than physical pleasure.

The realisation hit me hard. It was *almost* the 'jolt' that I needed to shake me out of this naughty behavioural pattern.

Yet there was another reason I wasn't fully comfortable in that environment.

'You've never fucked a hooker?' asked Jason, loudly, as if making sure everyone who understood English knew the situation.

'I've just never needed to,' I said, justifying my sheltered life.

'Yeah, 'coz you're a right player, ain't ya?' he said, amusing himself.

I needed to do this, to feel like a man again, a

man who desires women and their naked form and just fucking loves giving it to 'em hard! Even just to see if I could!

'I'm gonna do one,' I said, and necked the rest of my rum and coke.

'Good for you, bro, now don't just go for the first one that offers it. Take your time, there're loads to choose from.'

Just as Jason had told me to be choosy, I felt a light touch on my arm, and I turned to see a Romanian goddess. Anna introduced herself, told me I had very nice eyes, and asked if I'd like to buy her a drink.

I could hear Jason laughing beside me, but he may as well have been a thousand miles away. I was like a rabbit caught in the headlights when she pushed her near-naked body against me and put her lips just millimetres from my ear, I could feel her heat all over me.

'Yes,' I thought, triumphantly, I could feel a movement in my pants.

She was the one.

'So are you going to buy me that drink?' she asked, batting her eyelids at me.

'How about we just go and fuck?' I said.

I heard Jason laugh out loud, spitting out drink as he did so, as Anna took me by the hand and led me up the stairs to her private room.

Sarah was at Amine's apartment, lying on the bed wearing just her bra and knickers. She had an unopened condom in her hand, squeezing the packet with her forefinger and thumb, digging her nails in, knowingly risking damage to the pregnancy prevention aid.

Amine was talking in Arabic on the phone, and it sounded like an argument, but Sarah could never tell if he was being aggressive when he spoke his preferred language, the language he spoke when he didn't want her to understand it. All his friends who spoke it were very animated when they used it too, perhaps it just sounded harsh to untrained ears, but then Amine ended the call rather abruptly and threw his phone on the bed and Sarah knew he wasn't happy, a common occurrence recently.

He looked at Sarah in her underwear, grabbed a T-shirt from a chair and threw it at her.

'Cover up,' he said, before adding something in Arabic that Sarah could only assume was an insult.

She tossed the T-shirt away, and stood up. As Sarah was putting her clothes on, Amine re-entered the bedroom carrying a sports bag and placed it in the bottom of the wardrobe.

'What's in the bag?' she asked.

'That's not for you to worry about,' he answered, not even glancing in her direction.

Sarah could feel the love of her life slipping further away from her, and it scared and upset her. She'd already lost one important male figure in her life, her dad, and she wasn't prepared to see this one walk out on her.

Amine walked out of the room again and Sarah heard him close himself in the bathroom.

She knew she shouldn't betray his trust, but Amine had been acting so out of character lately. He was stressed, obviously, but she catching the brunt of it, and she wanted to know what was going on.

She tip-toed to the wardrobe and lifted up the flap at the top of the bag. Inside were bundles of money, notes neatly piled and banded together.

The toilet flushed and the door to the bathroom opened. Sarah had moved away from the wardrobe and towards the door as Amine walked back in.

She picked up her bag.

'Where are you going?' he asked.

'Well, you obviously don't want me here tonight,' she said, still upset at the rejection of sex, 'so I'm going home. Call me when you're in a better mood.'

She kissed him on the cheek and brushed past him as she left.

I was lying naked on the bed, Anna on her knees on the floor, playing with my cock and balls, using her hands and mouth, but to no avail.

'Why are you not getting hard for me?' she asked. 'Do you not find me attractive?'

'Of course I do,' I said, 'I don't know what's wrong.'

I watched as she shook her head, unimpressed at my inabilities.

'You have taken the Cocaine?' she asked.

'Maybe a bit, but not much,' I lied to her. Incredibly, I was feeling ashamed of my bad habits in front of a hooker.

'Why you take Cocaine? Is it not more fun to

fuck?'

'Good questions,' I thought, 'I wish I had the answer.'

'I'm sorry, baby, maybe another time will be better,' she continued, a little upset that there would be at least one unsatisfied customer that night. I do like a girl who takes pride in her work. I could see she was getting frustrated, and then her phone alarm went off, my time was up, and my penis wasn't.

That was seventy euros for half an hour of total embarrassment. Lesser men would have bolted, not looked back, gone to another bar and drunk so much until they'd completely forgotten the ordeal.

But I am not lesser men. I am a glutton for punishment.

I wiped the sweat from my forehead, leant over the side of the bed and slid my hands into my jeans pocket. I fumbled around until I found another seventy euros and tossed it onto the table next to the bed, where my previous payment lay.

'Are you sure?' she asked, almost pitifully.

'Go on,' I said. 'Try sucking it again.'

And she did, for another half hour, with no end product.

Finally we were home, and Jason crashed out straight away. As normal, I was still a little higher than I should have been.

Lying on my bed, my hands were in my pants, doing everything and anything to provoke a positive reaction from 'Little Jimmy'; rubbing my bits, cupping my balls, grinding away with my hips, but he wanted none of it. In fact, it seemed the more I invited him out to play, the more he retreated into hiding.

I couldn't get an erection, not even a semi.

I pulled my hands out of my pants and they pinged back into place, then I grabbed a tissue and wiped the snot dribbling from my nose.

Frustrated, I closed my eyes and counted to ten slowly, trying to calm the panic. I remember counting close to a hundred before drifting off to sleep.

15 – HAPPY

Things looked a whole lot brighter when I woke up the next morning, the sun was shining, I felt refreshed after what must have been a good night's sleep, and most importantly, I had morning wood. A super-strong erection that would have had me tugging away if I didn't need to piss.

I threw on a pair of joggers, picked up a T-shirt then walked awkwardly to the bathroom and waited impatiently for Little Jimmy to soften up a bit so I could drain the weasel.

I washed my hands and face and brushed my teeth, and I was happy, until I saw my skinny body in the bathroom mirror.

'I've got to start working out,' was a thought that ran through my mind, 'someday soon, maybe in a few weeks' time, or the month after next.' I had a bit of a six-pack showing, but knew that was due to lack of food meaning nearly no fat covering my body. It certainly wasn't down to my none-existent fitness regime.

I met Sarah in the hallway as we both headed to the kitchen.

I didn't know where to look when I noticed she was just a pair of skimpy knickers with her tight white T-shirt.

'Did your parents not tell you that drinking

from a glass is more socially acceptable?' asked Sarah, frowning at me for drinking straight out of a bottle of water from the fridge.

'Clearly not,' I said. 'Sorry, it felt like Ghandi's flip-flop in my mouth.'

She didn't get my analogy.

'I was extremely thirsty,' I added.

'Oh.'

I noticed her step closer to me, entering my personal space.

'God, I'd love to enter *her* personal space.'

'So how did it go last night?' she asked, then continuing sarcastically with 'Big time drug-dealers out on the town.'

'It's a bit early for comedy, Sarah. And speaking of drug dealers, where's your boyfriend this morning?'

I liked Sarah more and more at this point, not just sexually either. She was pretty cool, and the seemingly growing distance between her and Amine, plus the bizarre tension between her and Jason, meant she would speak to me more than ever before. I'd go as far to say that we had grown close.

'He's seeing a friend along the coast, apparently. Probably his ex-girlfriend, not that he'd ever admit it.'

'Uh-oh, trouble in the camp is there?'

'Mind your own,' she said. 'He won't be back until late tonight apparently. Did you need to see him?'

'I reckon its Jason's turn to be honest,' I said, hopeful. 'He may have organised something with him already, I don't know, I'm just an employee.'

She smiled.

'So, I'm assuming you've nothing to do today. How about you accompany me to my bar?'

There had been a couple of occasions when we'd spent a morning or afternoon together, and I liked it. I didn't need asking twice before accepting the invitation.

'I should probably have a shower first,' I said.

She leant close to me, I felt her hair lightly touch and tickle my neck and shoulder.

'I'd say you definitely need a shower,' she said, and then whispered into my ear, 'Do you need someone to scrub your back?'

At which point my erection made a quick return, however, it was short lived.

We heard Jason's bedroom door open and she stepped away from me.

'Morning, Sarah, Jimbo,' said Jason, as he entered the kitchen.

I laughed at the look of shock that appeared on Jason's face as he noticed Sarah's attire.

'Blimey, Sarah, you gonna put some clothes on today?' he said, giving me a strange glance, as if I was in the wrong in being in her presence when she dressed like that.

'I'm going for a shower,' I said, handing Jason the water bottle as I headed towards the door.

'Don't be long,' said Sarah.

'And you've got to meet Amine later,' added Jason. 'He's up the coast at the moment, but he'll be back about five, so be ready.'

I turned and saw the hurt look on Sarah's face. Amine had lied to her, and knew that she'd probably find out through me or Jason.

'The cash is in my bedroom,' Jason continued, 'I'll reckon we'll fucking clean up again tonight, bro. And if you sort your drug problem out, we'll be fucking retiring by the end of the season.'

'I haven't got a drug problem,' I said, which was met by an awkward silence between the three of us.

'Come the end of the season, you will be retiring,' stated Sarah, 'when all of your punters stop coming to Spain to spend their holiday money on Cocaine.'

'Alright smart-arse,' said Jason.

I left them to it and headed to the shower.

'So what are you up to today?' asked Jason.

'Wouldn't you like to know?' replied Sarah, leaving him alone in the kitchen and heading to her bedroom to get dressed.

All clean and dressed in light joggers, vest and my newest pair of flip-flops, I went into Jason's room to get the money for the drugs that it looked like I'd be buying and not Jason after all.

Jason was back in bed, fiddling with his mp3 player, as I picked up my pile of cash and the cigarette box with Amine's inside.

'James,' called Sarah from another room, 'Are you ready?'

'Yeah,' I called back. 'Just going to the bar, mate, have a good sleep,' I said to Jason.

'Cool,' he replied. 'And be careful, man. If Amine thinks you're fucking around with her, he'll cut your fucking throat.'

'Yeah, I realise he's not the nicest guy in the world, Jase,' I said, getting bored of his constant warnings about something that wasn't any of his business, 'but I'm hoping the fact I'm not banging his bird, means he'll let me live a little longer.'

I gave him a smug smile and a cheeky wink that didn't impress him, and then I left the moody Australian to it.

Sarah done the wages for her staff and I sat outside the door, soaking up the sunshine, slowly sipping a cold bottle of beer and reading the sport pages of an over-priced copy of The Sun. It costs two euros fifty in Spain, that's around two pound, and the ink is cheap and nasty and comes off easily all over your sweaty hands.

She finished what she had to do and came outside to sit with me. I put down the paper and gave her my attention.

'You gonna join me for a drink?' I asked.

'No, James. My body's a temple, don't you know?'

'It certainly is.'

She gave a little smile that let me know I hadn't overstepped the mark. Things were getting a little flirty in my opinion, but it's always hard to gauge what women are thinking, well it is for me anyway.

'So, I haven't got to meet your man for a few hours,' I said, 'you wanna do something?'

She stared out to sea, pondering over something that I'd maybe never know anything about. I studied the soft curves on her face, her skin glistening in the sunshine.

'Penny for your thoughts?'

'Well, as we've only got a few hours,' she finally replied, 'how about we go to the beach?'

'Ok, but I've got no shorts. We'll have to run by the apartment.'

'No, we won't,' she said, smiling. 'It's a nudist beach.'

She stood up, stretched out her arms and let out a small moan as she loosened herself up.

I looked up to her smile beaming down on me.

'Are you serious?' I asked.

'Yes,' she said. 'I have towels here we can take, unless you're too embarrassed, James. Are you going all shy on me?'

Instinctively, I looked either side of me, checking to see if Amine or Jason were there and if this was a test, but nobody was there, no-one we knew anyway.

'Fine, ok' I said. 'But if Amine hears about this, I'll kill you.'

She laughed.

'Not if he kills you first.'

We took Sarah's scooter and headed out of town to a nudist beach that up until five minutes before, I never knew existed. I was nervous about getting my clothes off in front of Sarah, excited about her getting her clothes off in front of me, and wondering where this was leading.

We arrived and I was glad to see the beach wasn't busy at all, in fact other than a few gay couples, I'm assuming pairs of men sunbathing nude together are homosexuals?, and the occasional naked old man walking his dog, we were pretty much on our own.

We found a secluded patch of sand, threw down our towels, and undressed, although disappointingly, Sarah kept her knickers on.

We laid ourselves down close to each other.

'So you've never been to a nudist beach before?' she asked, sniggering at my feeble attempt of hiding my manhood by crossing over one of my legs.

'I've never seen one in my life. And anyway, how come you get to keep your knickers on?' I enquired.

'Because I'm a lady, James, and those are the rules.'

'Rules my arse,' I said, trying to sound playful, but aware the disappointment had shown through in my tone.

I pointed to two Spanish men, nude except flip-flops, walking hand in hand along the beach down by the water.

'I mean, this isn't natural.'

I looked back at Sarah, who had now turned and was lying flat on her back. She moved her hair from her face then slowly let her fingers run down her neck, over her breasts and all the way down to her thighs.

'Actually, James, this is all natural,' she said, calmly, confidently.

I could feel butterflies going mad in my tummy.

'So,' she continued, 'how many times has Jason tried to warn you away from me so far?'

I chuckled.

'I get the impression that he fancies you.'

'Just a bit,' she exclaimed. 'Have you seen that ridiculous vase he bought me? I have to have it in full view or he gets upset.'

'Oh, ok then. That explains why he wanted to tear my head off when I nearly broke it one day,' I said. 'So he's not your type then?'

'Well, James, I'm not sure if I have a type' she said, as she turned back onto her side and faced me. 'Sometimes I just like what I see.'

I was beginning to get aroused and had to turn flat onto my stomach to hide the movement that was happening downstairs.

'What does that tattoo on your back say?' she asked.

'You've never seen it? It's just a little memorial for someone.'

'Can I look?' she asked, and then leaned over above me without waiting for my response.

She saw that my tattoo was in memory of my son.

'You had a child that died?'

I turned and looked her in the eyes.

'He was just a baby really. It was a car accident, icy road, he didn't stand a chance.'

She placed her hand on my back, caressing the spot which held my terrible memory. I thought I could see her eyes welling up a little, maybe it was the breeze making her eyes glisten.

'Do you want to talk about it?' she asked.

'Not really.'

She stared at me, deep into my eyes.

'How do you find living your life with secrets?' she asked, with soft, endearing words that covered my body instantly with goose-pimples.

'Keeping my mouth closed is easy,' I answered. 'It's the talking that normally upsets people.'

She reached out and lightly took the back of my head in her palm, pulling me close.

'Then stop talking,' she whispered, before placing her lips on mine, and sliding the softest tongue I'd ever felt into my mouth.

I thought I was in heaven, and then things got even better.

She took my hand and placed it on her chest, squeezing her breasts through my fingers. I heard her moan as we kissed, her breathing became heavy and I could feel the movement of her body, she was rocking her hips and took my hand down past the smooth skin of her stomach and pushed it into her knickers, placing my fingers on her clitoris as she began to gyrate at a faster pace.

I noticed another old man walking down by the waterfront, maybe he'd noticed us, maybe not, and I didn't care. Sarah was approaching orgasm, and I was hard as hell.

She grabbed me around the waist, pulled me on top of her, yanked her knickers to the side and then grabbed my cock and shoved me inside of her.

I didn't last long.

The excitement was too much for me to even try to delay the inevitable, but happily, she climaxed at the same time.

We shared a brief kiss as I lay on top of her, then she rolled me off and smiled.

'I think it's time for a dip,' she said, standing, and then pulling me to my feet before running off towards the sea.

16 – THE EPIPHANY

Things had gone pretty well at the club that night as well, and the day was looking to be the best I'd had in a long time.

I took a cab back the apartment with the last bag of Cocaine in my pocket, undecided as to whether I'd have any or not. I was still buzzing about shagging Sarah earlier on, it was a right result, and I'd been reminded that there are natural highs in life, highs which didn't involve putting toxins into your body via smoking or injecting or sniffing synthetic drugs up from toilet seats.

Clearly, there was an ever-so-slight risk of Amine finding out, but I couldn't believe she'd tell him. She loved him, in her own way, so wouldn't take the chance of telling him just to be 'honest' or 'truthful', those over-rated qualities that often damage relationships more than enhance them.

Plus, she mentioned keeping secrets, which all but guaranteed that her lips were sealed, and I knew mine were. I didn't fancy Amine or Jason finding out, I was quite happy knowing that I'd screwed the hottest woman in my life right now and also that my cock was fully functioning, albeit a little quick off the starting block.

Of course, things can change quickly in today's world, and as I climbed out of the taxi outside the apartment, I couldn't fail to notice Amine screech off in his car, driving past me with an angry look on his face. He didn't see me, and I was glad, as the look in his eyes told me that he'd just received some bad news.

Not that I didn't care about Sarah, but my first concern was for me.

I hoped, and even prayed a little to a God that I don't believe exists, as I walked up the steps to the apartment that Sarah hadn't come clean about us playing 'hide the sausage' at the nudist beach.

Nervously, I entered the apartment and emptied my pockets in my bedroom, before heading to the kitchen to get myself a drink. There was no sign of Sarah until I was making my way back to my room, and I heard her sobbing in her bedroom. I put my bottle of beer, only my third of the evening, down on my bedside table, and then made my way to Sarah's bedroom.

I tapped gently on the door, had no response and then opened it slightly and peered inside, not sure as to what to expect. I'd seen her upset and even angry before, but never crying.

No lights were on but I could see her outline on the bed under a blanket.

'What's up Sarah?' I asked, 'Are you alright?'

'Not now, James. Just leave me alone, please.'

I wanted to leave her alone. I wanted to go to my room, sip on my beer and fall asleep whilst watching a film on my laptop, but I felt obliged to show her that I was there for her.

'I saw Amine leaving,' I continued.

'Just fuck off, will you?' she yelled. 'Give me some space, please, for fuck's sake.'

'Ok,' I said, defensively, 'goodnight.'

I gently closed the door and heard her inhale sharply before crying louder than her previous sobs.

I retreated back to my room, relieved that I hadn't discovered that Amine was aware of what happened, but worried that it was still a possibility to be the case.

And that was when the moment of weakness arrived, and I racked up my first line of Coke of the evening. I washed down a cigarette with my beer and another line of Powder, only to realise that I wasn't high.

I wasn't sober, but a million miles away from the 'high' that I should have had after a couple of hefty hits of my drug of choice.

If anything, I felt a bit sad.

I sat in silence, thinking a lot of Sarah, and Amine, and if he knew or not. And then, of course, if he knew, that I'd be in the shit. And then Jason would find out, and I'd be in the shit with him as well.

I'd have the occasional moment of rational thinking, realising that if Amine knew, he'd have called me and threatened me, or even waited at the apartment for me to come home, perhaps even waited in my bedroom, sat in the dark with a knife in his hand to stab me to death or cut off my nuts when I came home too drunk, high and feeble to defend myself.

But then what was the problem?

Maybe they'd just reached breaking point in

their relationship, and today at the beach was just a coincidence. Although, regardless of her recent infidelity, she loved Amine, it was clear as day to see and nobody could deny it, even Jason, who I now knew had feelings for Sarah stronger than he'd ever let on.

I knew I had to stop being paranoid, but then again, what a situation to be in.

I didn't want to be caught up in this mess, and for the first time in months, I thought about going home. I looked at the wardrobe where my bag was stored and thought, 'what if I just packed up my things and went?'

It was at that moment I felt something running down onto my lip from my nose, and almost in auto-pilot, took some tissue from the draw and wiped the snot from my face, only this time it wasn't snot, it was another nose bleed, but the blood was pissing out, more than ever before.

I found myself in the bathroom, stood over the sink, with tissue shoved up my damaged nostril and pinching my nose in an attempt to stem the bleeding.

I looked up into the mirror, I looked ridiculous.

The bleeding seemed to have stopped, but my face was a mess, and also, glancing down at the reflection of my skinny body, I noticed how weak and feeble I'd become. I became incredibly self-conscious in the space of seconds. Any minute amount of 'high' that the Coke had given me was well and truly gone, and I had a sick, awful feeling in my stomach.

Late nights or no sleep, weight-loss, shady Moroccan drug dealers, crazy flat-mates and occasional impotence, 'What the fuck am I doing?'

And there it was, the moment of clarity, the epiphany that I'd done my best to avoid without realising it, the 'jolt' I'd needed to realise I needed to make an effort for change.

I didn't recognise that man in the mirror, and I didn't like who I saw.

I went to my bedroom and picked up the Coke, went to the window and ripped apart the plastic bag, letting the Devil's Dandruff fall freely into the dark of the night.

It wasn't quite the second natural high of the day that I was experiencing at that moment, more a sense of relief that was almost as good, but certainly more important.

If I forgot the money that I was enjoying spending on expensive clothes and food and alcohol, what did I have in my life? Fuck all.

I'd lost track of everything, somewhere, somehow, I was living a dream that wasn't mine. I didn't give a toss about money, not like that anyway, I wanted success more than anything, but I guess I misunderstood what success really was.

And what about the drugs? I thought I came here to get away from them, but I all too easily fell back into that lifestyle, without any real hesitation.

I saw that I'd left Hertfordshire because I wasn't happy with how my life was going, but it was now clear that I'd simply brought my problems with me, instead of facing them head on and working through them.

I could stop going to the pub, maybe go the

gym instead. Eventually I'd meet another girl, maybe have a kid or two.

What the fuck was I doing hanging out in pretentious clubs, selling drugs, being friends with a psychopath, with both of us infatuated with some bird who clearly has issues, as she can't tear herself away from a man who obviously doesn't want to commit?

I looked around the small room where I'd been hiding for the last few months, my bedroom, with absolutely no personal touches to it. There were no photos on display and my clothes were hidden behind wardrobe doors.

This could be anyone's room, but it wasn't mine.

I pulled down the window blind, laid myself down on the bed and switched off the lamp.

Complete darkness.

'This isn't my home. These aren't my friends. It's time to go.'

17 – ANOTHER NEW START?

I stirred in my bed, my phone vibrating on the table next to me, disturbing my slumber. I opened my eyes and immediately remembered my final thoughts last night.

Finally, things were going to change, I was ready. I knew what I wanted now, and psychologically, I was preparing for myself for another big change in my life. It meant a return to everything and everyone I knew and loved, but I would walk a different path, with goals I'd work to achieve, and hopes and dreams that kept me moving forward, not dwelling on the mistakes and pain of the past.

My phone stopped vibrating as I reached out to pick it up, then I heard what sounded like a cushion being thrown at the wall behind me. It was a morning wake-up call from Jason, although I couldn't remember asking for one.

I rolled out of bed and knocked on the wall, 'be there in a minute,' I called, and then headed to the bathroom to empty my bladder, brush my teeth, and wash my face. Then I inspected my nose, there was no visible damage.

I walked into Jason's room, nervous at the thought of telling him that I wanted no more involvement in the Coke business, or Cocaine at all come to mention it.

He was under the covers, tired and grumpy looking.

'What is it?' I asked.

'There's the money,' he said, nodding towards the bedside table as normal. 'You've got to meet Amine in about an hour.'

'You called him already?' I asked, knowing that this made things more awkward.

'Yeah, you know me, Mr Efficient.'

'Shit.'

My head dropped, chin making contact with my chest, my eyes weighing down on my eyelids. I could feel his gaze on me, and from somewhere, plucked up the courage to break the news.

'Please don't be a cock about this,' I begged him, silently.

'I want out, Jase,' I said. 'I don't want to do this anymore.'

He looked perplexed, and sat up on his elbows, turning towards me and giving me his undivided attention.

'Are you fucking serious?' he said. 'Did you sleep alright?'

I thought sincerity was the best option, you can't bullshit a bullshitter, and Jason was certainly one of them.

'Yeah, I'm serious, Jase. I'm falling apart, mate. Look at me, skin and bones, fucking nose bleeds,' I explained.

'Well, stop sniffing so much fucking Powder then.'

'Jase, if it's there, I'm gonna sniff it,' I

admitted. 'It's become a bit of a habit now and you know it.'

He adjusted himself in his bed, curling up and head back down on his pillow.

'I'm too tired to argue, James,' he said.

'James?' I thought. That was the first time he'd called me that without trying to be funny.

'We'll talk about this later, alright?' he continued, 'But I've ordered the gear now, so unless you want to call Amine to cancel, you'll go and meet him. And I wouldn't want to fuck him about like that. He was in a shitty mood already, for some fucking reason.'

'Shit.'

I'd forgotten about Amine, and what he knew, or might have known, and the anger I'd seen in his face last night.

Cancelling a drug order was a 'faux pas', or the equivalent in Spanish, and I didn't want to be the one to do it, so reluctantly I resigned myself to the fact that I was just going to have to be disciplined with regards to the Coke, as we'd made a commitment, and breaking it would mean more hassle than it was worth.

'Fine,' I said, 'but this is the last time, Jase. After this batch is gone, I don't wanna be involved anymore. It's over.'

'We'll see,' I heard him mutter to himself.

I collected the money and left the room, closed the door and leant against the doorframe, reassuring myself that I was in a better place in my head, and that this was the final time I'd have to do something like this.

I was on the home straight, soon to be heading

home with clear ideas about who I want to be and how I wanted to live my life. I wasn't going to go home rich like I thought I wanted, but successful in another way, in discovering what I truly wanted and valued, which were my family and friends, but also importantly, sobriety and a positive direction in life.

'Self-discipline, James, it all starts with self-discipline.'

I'd left the apartment pretty sharpish after a quick shower. I didn't want Jason changing his mind about wanting to argue my decision.

I thought about popping my head around Sarah's door and seeing how she was doing, but didn't want to risk her shouting at me either, especially with the angry Australian here.

I strolled along the promenade, went to a nice little bar and had a traditional English breakfast, with an orange juice and a small pot of tea. With a full belly, about the size of a large grape, I sat in the sunshine, occasionally glancing at my watch, until it was time to make a move.

It was the moment that would make or break my day.

Either Amine knew that I'd shagged his girlfriend, and he'd beat me down, or worse, maybe put me in his boot and get a gang of his mates to torture me and rape me and kill me slowly.

Or, he didn't know, and he'd just be the bullying prick that he'd always been and I'd take his lip for the sake of an easy life but content in the fact that soon these people and this situation would just be in my memories, which I would try my hardest to forget.

I stood in the car park, in my usual spot, nerves building no matter how hard I tried to convince myself that things were going to be ok. And then his car arrived, and as it drew closer, I saw that it was full of his comrades.

My stomach sank.

He pulled up a couple of metres away from me, and for the first time at one of our meets, Amine reached down to his side, opened the door and got out of the car.

'Oh shit.'

He walked towards me, and I noticed that he didn't look a hundred per cent, like he hadn't slept well, I almost thought that he'd been crying, but that didn't sound like the Amine I thought I knew.

He reached into his pocket, and I half expected a knife to be pulled out and pinned into my chest or throat, and I froze. But it wasn't a knife he pulled out, it was a cigarette carton, as usual with the Coke inside, which he gave to me and then asked me for the money, as he lit a cigarette that he took from behind his ear.

I gave him the cash without saying a word.

He was upset and I could see it, something had changed. I wondered if he could sense the change in me, in my awkward behaviour in front of him, or perhaps that my nervousness in his company up until this point had been a good thing, as it may have seemed to him that this was just me, 'Nervous Jim', the English junkie.

I put the Trumpet in my pocket, nodded, and

thanked him, before turning and making a move away.

'Wait,' he said.

I turned around, consciously keeping a safe distance between us.

'Jimmy,' he said, pronouncing my name with bitterness on his tongue, 'how long are you stayed in Marbella?'

I guess he meant how long had I been here, not fully understanding his English.

'A few months,' I answered, 'maybe four months. Why's that?'

Why did he ask? I really didn't know. I don't think he really knew, either, he just wanted to look at me I think. He was looking deep into my eyes, not in a sexual 'I fancy you' way, but as if he was trying to read my mind, trying to understand me, maybe.

Considering this was still a drug deal, it was strange to feel relieved when a police car pulled into the car park and Amine made his way back to his motor, then pulled away, giving me a nod and disappearing with his band of not-so-merry men.

I wasn't sure, but I think I'd just passed some sort of test with Amine.

I couldn't relax just yet though, as the policemen had parked their car and were getting out of the vehicle. I was getting closer to them as I walked toward the exit and could feel the Cocaine bulging in my pocket.

It was as I got level with the car that my heart skipped a beat. I saw one of the policemen had a dog with him. The Alsatian was taking a shit between the police car and another vehicle, and both the policemen stared at me as I passed.

'Is that a fucking sniffer dog?' I thought. 'Thank fuck he's otherwise engaged.'

They didn't stop me, or say a word. One of the coppers even gave me a tip of his cap and I guessed that they'd stopped to let the dog do his business, and maybe they felt awkward as I'd caught them letting it shit in a public place. Not that I cared, that was the last time I'd be in that car park. The coppers could have pulled down their pants and left their own 'number twos' if they wanted to.

I nodded back to them and smiled, feeling more relaxed with every step I took away from them. Perhaps the dog knew what was in my pocket, but was too busy doing what needed to be done. Nobody's perfect.

As I got out of view, I took to trotting briskly along the road, until I was a couple of blocks away and I felt my phone go off in my pocket, it was Sarah.

'Hey you,' I said. 'How are you doing today?'

'I'm fine, James,' she answered, sounding a lot better than the last time I'd heard her voice.

'So, what are you up to?' I asked, acting like the carefree friend I assumed she wanted me to continue being.

'I'm at the bar, one of the girls called up sick and I couldn't get any cover,' she said, 'actually, are you busy? It's just that I wanted to talk to you.'

'Yeah, talk?' I said, thoughts running through my head as to what the subject of conversation would be. 'No worries. I'm already pretty close. I'll be with you in a bit.'

'Ok, I'll treat you to a beer,' she said.

'No, not for me, thanks,' I told her. 'My body's a temple, don't you know?'

'See you in a bit, James.'

18 – FAVOURS CALLED IN

I was sat down, placing coasters, hanging them over the edge of the table, then flicking them up and trying to catch them. After a few goes I'd got it sussed, and started flipping four then five then more coasters at a time.

Sarah approached from behind and placed two coffees on the table before sitting beside me.

'You know, there were some kids in here earlier, playing that same game,' she said, dryly.

'Sorry.'

I pulled my coffee close and ripped open two sachets of sugar at once, tipped them in and stirred. She did the same.

'So,' I said, 'what did you want to talk about?' I asked.

That same dreadful feeling about Amine came over me again, even though I was ninety-nine per cent sure I was in the clear for now, but unless Sarah wanted to talk dirty in my ear and arrange for another session of secret sex, I had no idea what she wanted to say.

Things weren't awkward between us; there was no need to clear the air or anything like that.

'Obviously, nobody knows about our day at the beach, James,' she said, keeping her voice low, understandably.

'Good.'

'But Amine and I are having a few problems at the moment,' she continued, 'and I'm worried that he might start taking it out on you and Jason.'

I nodded my head, as if to understand what she was getting at, and I'm not sure why, because I didn't.

For me, if Amine didn't know that I'd shagged his bird, then there's no reason for him to take anything out on me. Unless he was uncomfortable with the fact that me and Jason were two horny, young men who both lived under Sarah's roof, which was more understandable, except he could have acted on that any time over the last few months.

But then, he was acting strange in the car park.

'It's funny you should say that,' I said, 'he was acting a bit weird a minute ago. So what's the crack?'

She blew into her coffee, took a sip and placed it back onto the table. For the first time since I'd met Sarah, she couldn't look me in the eye as she spoke.

'I think it's the end of the road for us. He doesn't want me anymore,' she said.

She was upset, and that was what I expected as I heard the news, as I knew that although Amine was an arrogant bastard, who didn't treat Sarah as well as most men would have, she loved him, in her own way, even adored him.

But it wasn't just hurt that I saw in her eyes as they looked out the door of her bar and towards the sea that glistened under the sun, it was anger. And it was definitely anger that made her clench her fists under the table, too.

That was another first that I'd witnessed in Sarah that day, a negative energy she was carrying. She was trying her best to hide it beneath her calm, warm and friendly exterior, and I wondered then how much of Sarah I really knew.

She moved a hand across to mine, squeezed it in hers, then looked across at me and forced a smile.

'I can trust you, can't I, James?' she said.

I decided now wasn't the time to tell her that the night before, I'd committed to the idea of packing my things and leaving all this madness behind, with the hope of never seeing any of them ever again.

'You know you can,' I said, realising I must have learnt something from those lying sons of bitches' at the telemarketing office.

'Amine has got my money,' she said. 'And I need it back.'

'What money?' I asked, surprised.

'My money,' she continued, 'About twenty thousand.'

Clearly there was more to Sarah and Amine's relationship than I imagined. Were they in business together? Did they have 'projects' other than a bar and selling drugs?

'He looks after it for me,' she said.

This was another surprise, because this implied that it wasn't a business, legit or otherwise, that they were into together, but that she had that sort of cash available for herself, so I really must have missed something.

I knew she had the bar and the apartment, but

other than that, it turns out I didn't know much about Sarah at all.

She told me it was kept in a sports bag in a wardrobe in his apartment, and asked me to get it for her. She said Jason would go with me, but I wasn't too keen to get involved at this point.

'Have you actually just asked him to give it back?' I asked, hoping a little diplomacy would stop me having to make quite possibly another wrong decision in my life.

'You don't really know him, James,' she stated, correctly. 'We're finished and he thinks he owes me nothing. He won't give it back to me.'

Sarah was again avoiding my gaze, cleaning her nails or staring out to sea. She went silent at this point, which is a sales technique, leave the conversation hanging, the weaker person being the first to break the silence and almost always being dominated in the rest of the negotiation.

Of course, I was the weakest link.

'Ok, so how?' I asked. 'Do we just knock on the door and ask for it? I'm not sure he's gonna take much notice of me, or Jason, especially Jason.'

'I have a key,' she said. 'Go with Jason, let yourselves in and get the bag, my bag.'

I sighed, and she heard.

I knew that she knew I didn't want to do it, and she knew that I knew that she wasn't impressed by my reluctance to get involved.

'Then why can't you just go round when he isn't home?' I asked, rather fairly, in my opinion.

'I can't go back there,' she said. 'The last time I was there he threatened me, and pushed me around.'

'Well, it's all coming out of the woodwork now,' I thought. 'Sarah doesn't seem the sort to let herself get pushed about.'

And then, as if to prove my point, she turned to me and gave a stern look.

'I did you a big favour letting you stay with us, James, remember?' she said, not so much asking as reminding. 'You owe me.'

Not one to be bullied, I didn't cave in as quickly as she might have liked. I sipped the last of my coffee, and took my turn at staring out to sea.

'When?' I asked, cool as a cucumber.

'Tomorrow,' she said. 'He goes to the gym most mornings, so it's probably best to do it then.'

'And Jason is fine with this?' I asked, for some reason, maybe to delay any firm commitment on my part, as I was one hundred per cent sure Jason would have done this with his hands tied behind his back and blindfolded if she'd asked him to.

'Of course, *he'd* do anything for me,' she confirmed, and I did catch the inflexion in her voice as she said it, which I found childish, and not encouraging nor convincing as I imagine she mistakenly expected.

'I don't know, Sarah,' I said, 'I've got so much going on in my head at the minute. Just let me have a think about it.'

I patted her hand gently then stood. She grabbed my arm and gave a last desperate plea for help.

'If you do this, James, I'll owe you forever.'

'Thanks for the coffee,' I said, and left.

19 - DECISIONS MADE

Back in the cyber café, I took the piece of paper I'd just printed, from the guy from behind the counter, checked it all looked ok and smiled happily.

'Gracias,' I said, as I looked up to the owner and smiled at him, too, but he just wanted paying for the use of his internet and printer, and held out his hand for some cash.

'Y teléfono, por favour,' I continued, pointing toward my usual booth.

I sat down and misdialled, due to the excitement of the news I was about to break. I dialled again, and then my sister answered her phone.

'Hello.'

'Alright, sis? It's me.'

'Hey, James, long time no speak,' she said, joy in her voice. 'How are you doing? Are things ok?'

'Yeah, I'm fine, cheers,' I said. 'Listen, Esther, I'm just letting you know that I'm coming home.'

'Really, when?'

'Tomorrow,' I continued, 'I just booked my flight.'

'Tomorrow?' she said, with disbelief in her voice, making me wonder if she'd written me off. 'Mum'll be so pleased to see you,' she continued, 'and Finley, too, you know he doesn't stop talking about you.'

'Bless him.'

'So, I guess this is you fishing for a lift home, from the airport?'

'No, no I'm not, actually,' I explained. 'In fact you won't see me for a couple of weeks yet. I'm going back to rehab.'

Suddenly her tone changed.

'I thought you were already off that poison?' she said, steel in her voice.

My weekly phone calls to mum had even convinced Esther that I was sorting my life out. I was glad that I wouldn't have to lie anymore, especially to those that loved me like only my family did.

'Es, I know,' I reassured her, 'and I'm off it, I'm off it all. But I think a couple of weeks in rehab will do me the world of good. I'm thinking of the longer term. Do you know what I mean?'

'It didn't help before,' she said, quite rightly.

'But I'm ready for it now,' I replied. 'These fucking drugs... I'm ready to move on.'

There was a moment of silence.

That sales technique, where the first to break the silence was the weaker, ran through my mind. If I spoke first, she would think I sounded desperate, maybe even pleading for her to believe me. If she piped up first, then I'd take it as a sign that she trusted me, that she had faith that I was finally controlling, or at least trying to take control of my life.

'You know, that's the first time I've believed you when you've said that,' she said.

I wanted to say, 'I love you, Esther. And I'm doing this for you and Finley and Mum as much as I'm doing this for myself.'

But I settled with, 'It's the first time I've meant it. I'll see you soon.'

Jason was on his bed, eyes closed, screwing up his face as the vibrating phone beside him gradually woke him from his slumber.

He picked the phone up and squinted to see Sarah's name on the screen before answering.

'Hey, beautiful,' he said.

'Finally, where the fuck have you been?' came the voice from the other end of the phone line.

Jason listened as Sarah updated him on her morning meeting with 'that bastard, James' and informed him that 'the skinny Coke-head' didn't want to help out with retrieving the money.

Jason didn't seem too concerned about it, but Sarah was adamant, that if Amine was there when the collection was made, or came home during, then two bodies would be better than one.

Jason wondered if she really was concerned for his safety, or that she didn't trust him to do it alone, either messing things up or taking off with the cash.

'Jeez, alright,' said Jason, the high-pitched noises of a distressed woman stabbing at his eardrums, forcing him to interrupt, 'I'll sort it. He just needs a little convincing, that's all. Leave it to me.'

He ended the call and rolled over on his bed, trying to find that wonderful comfort that one always has when waking up, but sometimes struggles to find when trying to get to sleep in the first place.

'How the fuck am I gonna get that little English prick to grow a pair, and do as he's fucking told?' he thought to himself, probably in an Australian accent.

Jason woke up, this time naturally, with no phone vibrating against the wood of his bedside table, and now sat on top of that bedside table, were the weighing-scales and a bag full of smaller bags of Cocaine inside.

I was in my bedroom packing my suitcase, when I heard Jason stomp down the hallway and try to open my door.

It was locked from the inside.

'Hang on a second, mate,' I said, 'I'm getting dressed.'

I closed up the case and put it back in the wardrobe, looked at my reflection in the mirror, and nodded at myself, happy with the decision that I'd made.

I had butterflies in my tummy, excited about going home maybe, but also enjoying the added excitement of doing things secretly.

I didn't want to hear the bullshit from Jason about leaving him without a business partner, or anymore of this stealing back the stolen money from Amine. I didn't want a part of any of it, but I knew that the easiest way out was to just sneak off without saying a word.

Some might call it a coward's way out, but I didn't care. The important thing was that after one more night selling Powder, I was a free man, in body, mind and spirit. And I loved the feeling, it was another natural high, nearly as good as sex, which I'd promised myself to make an extra special effort to be involved with again in the very near future.

I opened the door to let Jason in, but he remained outside, stood in his work clothes.

I wondered if he was going to lecture me about not agreeing to help Sarah, or nag me about wanting to get out of the Coke game.

But he didn't.

'Alright, Jimbo?' he asked, 'I'm off in a minute mate. You got some Coke or you need me to leave you some?'

'I'm fine, mate,' I replied. 'You keep hold of it.'

'Alright, yeah, cool,' he said.

There was a moment when we caught each other's gaze, and for those two or three seconds, which felt like a lifetime, I swear I could hear the cogs of his brain turning, thinking up something, what I don't know, but I did know, or at least I thought I knew, this was the first time that Jason hadn't just came out and said to me whatever it was that he was thinking.

He had a couple of reasons to be unhappy with me at this moment, with the Coke and Sarah, but I guess the fact we had more Coke to sell tonight, meant he had to keep our working relationship intact, for the time being anyway.

It was an awkward moment, horrible really, and so another moment that confirmed to me I shouldn't be there. In that sense it was good, but still uncomfortable.

'Seeya in a couple hours,' he said, before turning and walking away.

I sat down on my bed, in near silence, and listened as he went to the kitchen, grabbed some water and food to take with him, and then open the front door and leave.

Then I stayed motionless in my room for a few minutes more, making sure he really had left, or didn't change his mind and come back in for an argument. Then I stood, pulled out my suitcase one more time and finished packing my things.

Everything packed away, the suitcase went back into the now empty wardrobe, and the door was closed.

I was happy, until I felt a familiar sensation on the top of my lip. I headed to the bathroom to fix my bleeding nose.

20 – DIFFERENCE OF OPINION

I arrived at the club around the usual time, got searched by the security who knew me by now, but didn't seem to care or realise why or how I could always be here spending. Perhaps they thought I was just another of these rich-boys out spending their super-rich fathers' money. Whatever, it didn't matter. It was the last night I would be seeing them, and what they thought of me was irrelevant, as long as they didn't catch me selling drugs that is, but they'd been so far off the radar thus far, that I hadn't been worried about them since the first week of our business venture.

I walked into the main bar and saw Jason chatting to a colleague. He saw me lingering in his line of vision in the background, and when he noticed me, I walked into the toilets and he followed.

As always, we made the exchange under the partition of two cubicles and flushed the loos and washed our hands at the sinks.

This was the moment he chose.

'So, you've spoken to Sarah today?'

'Yeah,' I said.

'And what d'ya think?'

I brought some of the cool water up to my

face. It was always hot in Trikki Beach Club, even in the toilets.

'I don't want any part of it,' I said, for some reason thinking a little honesty would convince Jason that it was unfair to push me into something that wasn't really any of my business.

'Oh, you don't?' he said, that aggressive nature of his taking no time at all to rear its ugly head, 'And you don't think you owe her a little something for taking you in?'

'I thought that's what the rent money was for,' I said, before turning my back on him to grab a paper towel and dabbing dry my face.

I half expecting the lunatic from down-under to jump me from behind and rip the head from my shoulders.

He didn't.

'Funny,' he said, rather calmly, bizarrely. 'And you're happy that Amine is stealing her money?'

'So she says,' I responded, immediately regretting it. Disrespecting Sarah to Jason was like waving a red rag to a bull.

'Are you calling her a liar?' he yelled, finger pointing at me and taking a step towards me.

I held my hands up, gesturing for him to calm down.

I was getting cocky, knowing that I was leaving soon, and risked getting a kicking for upsetting the people that, in their own way, and for whatever reasons, however selfish, had helped me when I needed it in the recent months.

'Listen, Amine might be an arsehole, a bully, even,' I explained, 'but he's played it straight with me from day one. He hasn't done a thing wrong to me, or you, for that matter.'

'Oh, he will,' said Jason, the anger in his voice making him sound desperate. 'Without Sarah keeping him cool, he could jump us at any time.'

It was strange that he said that, and maybe I should have realised then that I didn't fully appreciate the situation that I was in. In my eyes, I was on the home straight with my flight booked and my bag packed.

I didn't envisage anything happening to thwart my plan of escape.

'Well, with respect, I'll cross that bridge when I come to it,' I said, and walked out of the men's room, leaving Jason shaking his head whilst drying his hands, disappointment, anger and rage plastered across his face.

The club was packed and business was booming. Less than three hours into it and nearly all the Charlie had gone.

I was getting hungry and sipping on nothing but water all night was boring and tasteless, but I was determined to keep myself in check, stay sober and keep the promises I'd made.

'This time tomorrow I'll be back in the UK, home' I thought, with a clear idea as to what is important in life.

It was all going to plan, until another dribble of blood flowed from my nose and settled on my top lip. I made way to the toilets, head facing down, and not wanting people to see the blood. People liked seeing claret, psychopaths aside, but not the typical club-goer trying to enjoy their night out in an upmarket establishment such as this.

Holding tissue to my nose, I pulled out my phone and checked for any messages or missed calls as I stepped out of the toilet cubicle. Suddenly, I felt cornered, shadows came over me, and I looked up to see four Moroccans surrounding me.

'We want money,' said the Northern African, in pigeon English, 'we want Cocaine.'

I knew they weren't requesting to buy drugs from me, and they weren't looking for a hand-out or donation of money so that they could eat or feed their family.

I was being mugged.

I looked over the shoulder of one of the Moroccans and saw two European-looking guys feeling awkward, understanding the situation, but deciding to shuffle out of the men's room, when gestured to do just that by a couple of my aggressors.

'Shit.'

'I don't know what you're talking about, mate,' I said.

My hands went up, gesturing for calm again, could it work twice in a night?

No.

I'm not really sure what happened next, not exactly anyway, or for how long it lasted.

I remember the first few punches, then falling down but being held up at the same time. My phone was knocked out of my hand and I think I heard it slide off into one of the toilet cubicles, and then I remember being on the floor, getting kicked and stamped on, and finally waking up, cowering behind a toilet.

I didn't feel very good.

I sat up, examined myself as best I could, stood and hobbled to the sinks and looked in the mirror.

My face was battered, with a bit of blood here and there, and a couple of grazes and some red marks that would soon turn into full-blown bruises. I also had spit on my head and shirt which disgusted me, so I wasted no time in getting water all over my skin to clean myself, then dabbing spit and blood from my clothes with a wet paper towel.

'Fucking arseholes.'

It was only then that I realised that I'd been robbed as well.

I found my wallet on the floor where I'd been knocked out, but that cash had gone, around a hundred I think I had, and the last couple of bags of Coke were gone from my pocket, too.

On the plus side, I found my phone on the floor, a couple of cubicles along, but it looked broken. I kept it, for whatever reason, maybe it could be repaired, or maybe it couldn't. At that point my head still wasn't fully with it.

I'd stopped bleeding and after a final dab here and there with a fresh paper towel, I left the men's room and made my way to the bar.

'Jeez, mate, what happened to you?' asked Jason, surprise on his face.

'You got some cash for a taxi home?' I asked.

'Yeah, of course, man,' he answered, looking round for his superiors before pulling out a few notes from his pocket and handing them over.

'What happened?' he persisted.

'I just got jumped by some Moroccans in the toilets,' I explained. 'I think they knew I've been serving up.'

'Shit, mate, what did they say?'

I wasn't in the mood for talking about it.

'Look, I gotta go, I'll see you at home,' I said.

I turned and walked towards the exit, through the crowd of people dancing and drinking, all of whom were so high or drunk or caught up in their own worlds that they didn't notice the state I was in.

The security guards turned a blind eye as I walked past them and out of the club, it seemed like nobody wanted to know.

I was happy to see some taxis waiting, as hanging around made me nervous. I didn't know where these guys who just mugged me were, but I knew that I didn't want to run into them again, although in all honesty, I'm not sure if I'd recognise them if they were stood in front of me in broad daylight.

I got in the taxi at the front of the queue.

'Marbella Centro, por favour.'

I tried my phone, but the screen was cracked and it didn't work. I shoved it back in my pocket and realised the driver of the taxi was banging on about something. Of course, my Spanish was still hopeless, but I think I got the occasional word and the general message was understood.

'English people are pieces of shit.'
'Always fighting like animals.'
'No respect.'
'Happy I was hurt.'

All day I'd been dreaming of grabbing my bag

and saying goodbye to Sarah's apartment, my home for the last few months, but right then, I just couldn't wait to get back there and out of this taxi.

The four Moroccans approached the bar.
    Jason picked up a bottle of water, pulled a two hundred euro notes from his pocket and wrapped it around the plastic water-bottle, then handed it over to the leader of the Moroccans and grinned.
    'Thanks, bro. You guys have a good night.'

21 – CHANGE OF HEART

I woke up to Jason shaking me by the shoulder.

'Dude, dude,' he said. 'Looks like they did you in pretty good, mate.'

I slowly sat up, and swung my legs around to put my feet on the floor. Sitting in my boxer shorts, I took a look at my body and arms and legs and noted that the bruises had come along quite nicely, dark blue and black like bruises should be.

I could feel muscles aching as I picked up the box of painkillers from the bedside table and took out two tablets, chucked them into my mouth and washed them down with the last of the bottled water I had next to the bed.

'How's my face?' I asked.

He shook his head.

'Not great, mate,' he said. 'How ya feeling?'

'Fucking fantastic,' I replied, sarcastically of course. 'Is Sarah home? What time is it?'

'It's just gone seven. I think so, yeah, you want me to take a look?'

'Yeah, please. I couldn't find any plasters and stuff last night.'

'Plasters? I think you might need stitches, mate,' he said, grinning, as he headed off to Sarah's bedroom.

I yawned and began to stretch but had to stop

due to the pain. I took a good look at my face, thought how butch it made me look, then put on a pair of jeans, grabbed a T-shirt and made my way to the front room.

I slowly eased myself down onto a chair by the dining table as Jason appeared with a tired-looking Sarah following behind.

'Oh, James, what happened?' she asked, visibly shocked by the sight of my battle wounds, 'Who did this to you?' she continued.

'I don't know.'

'He wants some plasters,' said Jason, to Sarah.

'We need to get you to the hospital,' she said to me.

'No, it looks worse than it is,' I said. 'Please, Sarah, can you just clean the cuts for me? And cover them maybe?'

She had to tear herself away from staring at my face and headed to the kitchen. She was back in moments with the first aid box that I spent half an hour looking for the night before yet couldn't find. She knelt down beside me and began looking through the different bottles and boxes in the medical box.

'You know who's behind this, don't ya?' asked Jason, not to anyone in particular.

'I'd never seen 'em before' I said.

'You said they were Moroccans. And they knew you were selling Powder. How hard did they hit you on the head, Jimbo?'

I winced at the pain, as Sarah dabbed away at a cut above my eye, with cotton wool that must have been drenched in surgical spirit or something similar. I didn't know what it was, I didn't even look. It seemed at my weakest I trusted her to take care of me.

Had I been too quick to decline the help she had asked of me?

'Sorry,' she said, softly, 'this is going to hurt.'

I stared into her beautiful eyes as she cleaned my wounds and covered them, showing nothing but tender, loving care as she did so.

'So what d'ya wanna do about it, mate?' Jason continued on in the background.

'Amine, you bastard, why did you need to do this to me? I never did a thing done wrong to you,' I thought.

The need to avenge my unfair beating ran through my blood.

I never pretended to be a hard man, but I'd grown up knowing that sticking up for yourself was the bare minimum a man should do. Maybe it was a bit late for that, and revenge was just revenge, but I was angry with Amine, I didn't deserve this.

Coupled with the guilt that was creeping into me about not helping Sarah, a woman who had let me into her home, and now cared for me when I needed it, I made a decision, and changed my mind over the previous decision I'd made.

Of course, I'd still be catching that flight later that day, and it'd still be a secret, but the least I could do was to help Sarah get back her money, now that I knew how much of a shit Amine really was.

'What time did you say he goes to the gym?' I asked.

'Around eight or nine,' she answered, a slight

smile appearing across her face, 'It depends on what time he gets up.'

I looked up to Jason, who sported that cheesy grin so effortlessly across his face, even at stupid o'clock in the morning after working all night.

'So you're ready for this?' I asked.

He crossed his arms and puffed out his chest displaying his manliness, if that's your thing.

'I was born to do this shit,' he said. 'But why wait until he goes out? He needs teaching a fucking lesson if you ask me?'

'Nobody's asking you, Jason,' interjected Sarah. 'All I want is my money and him out of my life.'

Sarah finished dealing with me and packed away her medical kit, then took it back to the kitchen.

'I'm gonna get changed, get ready, then we're gonna do this shit,' said Jason, the violence already in his voice.

Maybe he was right. Maybe he was born to do this shit.

I put the rest of my clothes on, and laced up my trainers tight because I thought that I'd maybe be running away from someone at some point. Flip-flops were a definite no-no today.

I walked into the kitchen and stood beside Sarah, as she poured a generous glass of whiskey.

'It's a bit early for that isn't it?' I asked.

'Actually, it's for you,' she said, 'I thought it might help with the pain.'

She was probably right, and to be honest, I imagine it would have helped with the nerves also. I feared the worst about Amine being there with his friends and all sorts of shit kicking off.

'Not for me,' I said, 'I'm on a bit of a detox.'

'Good for you,' she said, before drinking half of it herself. Apparently I wasn't the only one nervous.

She told me that she wouldn't have asked if there was any other way, if there was anyone else she could have turned to, and that sending Jason in on his own would have been a bad idea, which I didn't disagree with.

I told her it was fine, admitted that I owed her for helping me, that I was sorry for not agreeing to help at the first instance, and that breaking into a gangster's apartment to steal money from him was the least I could do.

Always try and inject a little humour into your life.

We'd shared a bit of a rollercoaster ride over the last couple of days, between the sex, her shouting at me, asking for help with me rejecting her, her cleaning my wounds and then me finally deciding to help her.

As we stood next to each other, she finished the whiskey, and I felt pleased that I wasn't going to let her down. It seemed that Amine had done enough of that already, and aside from her infidelity with me, she had been a great girlfriend to him, from what I'd seen anyway.

'This shouldn't take too long,' I said. 'Will you still be here when we get back?'

'I have to oversee a delivery at the bar, but it isn't a biggie,' she replied.

She picked up a set of keys from the kitchen

counter, a set that I hadn't seen before, and dropped them in my hand.

At least, technically, it wasn't 'breaking in.'

Jason still hadn't appeared, so as Sarah went back to her room, I sat back down on the same table chair in the front room. Lowering myself into the seating position, I was having second thoughts about having a whiskey, maybe taking the edge off things, as the painkillers either weren't strong enough or hadn't kicked in fully just yet.

My body was accustomed to Class A illegal, shit. This over the counter medicine didn't seem to cut it.

Just as I was growing weak-willed enough to drag myself up and back to the kitchen and the whiskey bottle, Jason walked into the front room and all my pain just disappeared in an instant. I put it down to the endorphins released throughout my body from the sheer joy I got from seeing how Jason was dressed.

He stood before me in army-style, khaki combat trousers, matching top and baseball cap. He even had shiny black boots, Doc Martins or similar, and he looked like he was ready for war.

'Fuck me, Jase, you been preparing for this for a little while?' I asked, laughing on the inside, but a little worried, too, as this young man stood in front of me clearly had issues.

'Bought it yesterday before work,' he said. 'Fucking nice, eh?'

'Yeah, it looks good,' I replied, seeing him cast an eye on my casual-wear and feeling somewhat underdressed.

GET CLEAN

He held up what seemed to be the heavy end of a pool cue and some cable-ties.

'Jesus Christ, help me now,' I thought, not a believer all of a sudden, more of a hoper.

'Let's do it,' he said.

22 – BEST MADE PLANS

It was about a fifteen minute walk to Amine's apparently, not that I'd ever been there, and in my current state, moving as slowly as I was, fifteen minutes in Jason's head probably was a lot further than fifteen minutes on my battered legs.

It did give me the re-clarify what my plan was for today, which now went, get Sarah's money, go home, get my money from last night's drug sales, wait for the opportunity to sneak out, and go.

The day didn't have to be long, or difficult. On the contrary, if Amine was out, as was assumed and hoped, then things were going to run smoothly, as long as the money was where Sarah said it was, and he hadn't moved it, or spent it, which would have been too bad but not my problem.

But that all relied heavily on Amine being at the gym, or anywhere else but at home, and Jason's eagerness to get this done, to put right what his great nemesis, 'that thieving fucking Arab' had done to the woman he adored, meant we were getting to his apartment earlier than made me comfortable.

'Slow down a bit, mate,' I said, 'I'm not in top form at the minute.'

He turned back to me, gestured for me to get a move on and carried on walking at the same speed as before, clearly not fussed if I didn't make it there at all.

'Did you notice Sarah being short with me back there?' he asked.

I didn't have the heart to tell him that I couldn't remember the last time she wasn't short with him.

I knew that Jason probably now thought he had a chance with Sarah, now that she was very much single and probably a little fragile, maybe even needy; always a great time to pick up a woman, and good luck to him, I'd be happy for them both, if I were to find out that was the case. Not that I had any intention of leaving them a way of letting me know.

So we arrived outside Amine's apartment block, and stood across the road. Jason was working himself up, as I looked up and down the road for Amine's car.

It wasn't there, but that didn't mean a thing. Parking must have been a nightmare around this area, the roads were packed, and with no allocated parking, it must have been a bit of a free for all.

From where we stood, even if a light was on inside his apartment, we'd not been able to see it, what with our line of sight, and also the reflection of the bright sky on the glass that far up the building didn't help.

'Let's go,' said Jason, and headed off towards the apartment block, keys in hand. Reluctantly, I followed.

Climbing the two floors wasn't easy with my aching legs, ribs, arms, neck and face, but I could feel the adrenaline kicking in, masking the pain. I was shaking a little, but fully alert.

This guy had gotten me beaten up last night, so even if he was there, I told myself that maybe he did deserve a slap or two, which would be coming from Jason, of course.

I stood back as Jason peeped in through the window, and then put his ear up against the door and listened for a moment before shaking his head at me, and pushing a key into the front door.

The key didn't turn. And then it got jammed in there. It took a good wiggle to get the key back out, this made a noise, and I was close to making a noise of my own in the back of my pants.

He tried another key, and slowly, quietly, opened the door.

He side-stepped inside through a narrow opening, and for a split-second, I thought about walking away and leaving him to it, but he looked back out at me and gestured for me to follow him in.

'Please, please, please, don't be home,' I begged Amine, through power of thought.

We tip-toed our way through his apartment, checking each room for the owner as we passed them. The kitchen was empty, then a small bedroom that was empty too, and a bathroom, also empty.

There was one room left, the only room hidden by a closed door.

'A closed door,' I thought, surely that means he's in there. He's tucked up in bed, maybe alone, maybe with someone else. Maybe Amine and his new girlfriend are in the middle of making sweet, sweet love and me and Commando Jason are about to interrupt and demand the money.

I felt like I was in a film. A good film, maybe, maybe the sort of film I'd like to watch, but certainly not a film I'd like to be based on parts of my life. I didn't want a character playing me, to have to be in this scenario, because that would mean that I'd have been in this situation, which is stupid, and I knew that as I watched Jason turn the handle on the bedroom door and push it open.

There was no sex. No movement at all. It was just Amine, asleep, on his own.

Jason made his way to the side of the bed and stood over the Cocaine supplier. He pulled out his cosh and looked ready to pounce if Amine made any sudden moves, then he nodded me towards the wardrobe, which I couldn't see at this point, as I hadn't been able to get my jelly legs to move my concrete feet through the bedroom door.

I took a deep breath, promised myself to never get involved in anything like this again in my life, then took fairy steps toward the wardrobe at the far side of the bedroom.

As I passed the bed, I noticed that Amine looked peaceful, and it didn't compute how he'd gotten those guys to beat me up the night before, it just didn't seem fair, or just, but he was a drug-dealer, and I guess I was just a junkie to him, even if I was a junkie who gave him chunks of cash every few days.

I reached the wardrobe and took the small handle in my grip, turned to Jason, and he nodded to the wardrobe door.

'Open it,' he said, quietly, but still too loud for my liking.

Amine hadn't woken, so after wiping the sweat from my forehead, I gently opened the door, and gave a sigh of relief when I saw the bag, just as Sarah had described, sat at the bottom of the wardrobe.

It wasn't zipped shut, so I bent down and lifted up a corner of the opening. There were bundles of money in that bag, and for a moment I felt like our mission had been successful, everything had gone to plan, except Amine being there, but he hadn't woken up and killed us yet.

And he wouldn't, either.

A cracking sound forced me to turn around, and there I saw Jason bringing down the pool cue again onto the head of Amine.

And then he did it again.

My stomach began to convulse, I had to gulp heavily to stop vomit from flying up my throat, out of my mouth and covering everything in sight.

'He looked at me,' explained Jason, an acceptable reason to him for smashing somebody's face in.

I didn't know if Amine had woken or not, I didn't hear anything before Jason attacked him. But I understood that if Amine did wake up, there wasn't much choice for Jason, but to be the first to make a move. It also didn't escape me, that even if our Arabic, drug-peddling, money-thieving enemy had opened his eyes and seen the excitable Aussie, he wouldn't have seen me, the timid Englishman, as he was facing the other way.

I needed to get out of there.

I grabbed the bag, zipped it up and made my

way out of the bedroom, looking back at Jason who still stood above Amine, breathing heavily, sweating, and with a devilish look across his face.

I glanced long enough at Amine, to see his face covered in blood and a gap in his teeth that I'd never noticed before. Clearly Jason had played dentist and removed a couple of teeth just moments ago. And I could see his chest moving too, he was breathing, which was good, and he was pretty much unconscious, as far as I could tell, which meant it was an ideal time to leave.

I waved a hand at Jason, beckoning him to come with me.

'It's all there?' he asked, pointing at the bag.

I nodded, refusing to talk in case Amine could hear me and know for sure who was with Jason, as if he would need to convince himself that dumb and dumber wouldn't be working together on this one.

'I reckon he must have some Powder 'ere,' he continued, looking smug as if that a good idea right now.

He prodded Amine in the face with the cosh.

'You got some Charlie, mate?' he asked him, 'You got some fucking Charlie?'

CRACK

THUMP

Twice more he brought that pool cue down on Amine's jaw. I've watched a few boxing bouts in my time, and I've seen professional fighters go wobbly at the knees from less force on their chins that that.

Amine was undoubtedly unconsciousness now, but at that point, Jason was the one I feared more. He had dribble coming from his mouth, like a rabid dog, his eyes were bulging and he had a throbbing vein ready to explode on the side of his sweaty forehead.

'Fuck this, Jase,' I said, 'Come on, for fuck's sake.'

'I'll meet ya downstairs.'

And with that, I left him to it. If he wanted to find some Coke that badly, he could do it on his own. If Amine was going to wake up, or if any of his friends knocked on the door, I didn't want to be there.

I peeked out from behind the front door, saw that nobody was coming or going along the corridor, and then stepped outside, closed the door and calmed myself down as I headed towards the stairwell.

I went down the stairs, out of the main door and about fifty metres along the road, as fast as I could with my damaged body, until I came across a bench to sit on.

There I waited, with the sun rising up from behind the clouds and gifting me warmth. I closed my eyes, counted to a hundred, and slowly brought my heart rate down to a normal level.

My nerves were settling, and the job was done, for my part anyway.

Jason was taking his time, being a greedy bastard. Maybe by taking the Coke as well, he was showing Amine that the tables had turned, and that he would no longer be playing the victim anymore, that it was his turn to be 'numero uno.'

It was coming to the end of the season, and in theory, Jason wouldn't need Amine in the future, he had all winter to source another drug-dealer if he wanted to carry on next year.

Also, if Jason really wanted Sarah to take notice of him, to see him as the main man, in the way that he understood she looked up to and adored Amine, then maybe he was taking this opportunity to do just that, like alpha males fighting over turf and women.

23 – ALPHA MALES

Amine's apartment was now a complete mess. Jason had gone through drawers and cupboards, tipped over plant-pots and finally found some Coke at the back of the freezer.

He held the cool, bag of Cocaine in his hand and weighed it up in his mind.

'About an ounce,' he thought to himself, before opening it up and taking a sniff. The petrol and chemical substance made his tummy go, he felt a movement and some bubbling, and although even Jason knew that taking time out to dump his load in his victim's home was not a good idea, when you need a Coke-poo, you need to go sharpish.

He sat on the toilet and within moments his bowels had emptied. He was so relieved that he didn't notice the sounds of someone regaining consciousness in the master bedroom.

Without washing his hands, the Australian was on a mission and went back to the kitchen, wiped the work-surface with one swoop of his arm and picked up the bag of Powder, then tipped out a few grams worth. He brought his hands together around the Coke, making it into a manageable pile, and then leant down, stuck his nose into it and inhaled sharply through both nostrils.

Half of the pile had gone, and as Jason stood up straight, he felt his jaw and both fists tighten as the rush of chemicals his body produced in response to the Cocaine ran through him.

He grinned, even giggled a bit as he reached into his pockets, searching for his cigarettes, and then cursed as couldn't find them. He must have left the at home.

He looked about the kitchen to see if Amine had left a packet lying around, but before he found any smokes, his eyes came across something potentially more dangerous than cancer-sticks.

He moved towards the large kitchen knife that lay on the draining board, shining in the sunlight that was breaking in through the kitchen window. He took it in his hand, brought it close to his face, inspected the blade and smiled.

Only Jason knows how his mind works, but anyone who had spent time with him, knew that the thoughts he had running through his head when holding a knife like that, with someone he hated just a few steps away from him, were not thoughts that a normal person would have.

His smile stretched into a large grin, the proverbial light bulb glowed above his head. He'd had an idea.

The grin disappeared as he stepped briskly towards the bedroom, knife in hand, and with a look as hard as steal on his face he marched up to the bed.

But then he was confused. And he turned around as heard the sound of metal on metal.

C-CLICK

Jason stood facing a battered Amine, standing

before him with a cocked-revolver pointed at his face.

'Shit,' said Jason, so high off the Coke, he probably didn't fully understand the gravity of the situation.

It was Amine's turn to smile, albeit through broken teeth.

'Lose the knife,' he ordered.

Jason laughed as he tossed it onto the far side of the bed, then crouched down onto his knees and faced the wall, as instructed by the man with the gun.

'You thought you'd get away with this?' barked Amine, 'Coming to my house, fucking my woman. You been fucking my woman?'

Jason squealed in pain as Amine landed an almighty kick in Jason's privates, his head crashed against the wall from the force, and he thought his testicles had moved from his scrotum all the way up to his stomach.

'And you take my money?' he continued, 'Where's my money? That English fuck has my money?'

CRACK

Another heavy kick, this time to Jason's ribs, that sent him sprawling onto his side. He was in agony and fighting to breath.

Amine picked Jason up by the scruff of the neck and tossed him onto the bed. He then climbed on top of the Aussie and yanked his arms behind his back, planted his knee on both of them with his full weight, pinning them down onto the spot and almost snapping the spine at the same time.

'You come to my house?' he yelled, 'You come to fuck me over?' Huh? You want to fuck me over? You want to fuck me?'

Amine yanked at Jason's cargo pants and pulled them and his underwear down.

'I'll show you,' he screamed into Jason's ear, dribble falling from his mouth.

He pushed the gun forcefully into the side of Jason's head. Somewhere under his hair you'd be able to find the perfect imprint of the tip of the barrel of a .38 Smith & Wesson handgun.

'I'll show you how to really fuck someone over,' he continued.

He grabbed Jason's throat, squeezed and pulled it up, leaning down on his knee. Jason was beginning to realise how helpless he was, and then things got worse.

Amine rammed the six-shooter into Jason's arsehole, tearing it and ripping the skin as it entered him.

Jason tried to scream but couldn't. The grip around his neck hardly allowed air through, let alone cries for help.

'You'll regret the day you fucked with me, you little bitch,' whispered Amine, almost calmly, as he worked the gun in and out and in and out of Jason's body. 'You like that? Huh? You little faggot, you little fucking faggot.'

As most people would at this point, Jason thought it was over, that there was no way out. But then he had a touch of luck; the knife, it was on the bed and he could see it. The pain and humiliation suddenly fell silent in his head, and he focused on that knife, sat a couple of feet away from him.

He could see that knife still shining, even in the dimly lit bedroom, maybe it was the glow of an angel offering the knife back to Jason, 'Save yourself.'

'You like that?' continued Amine, enjoying his actions more by the second, 'you like that, you little bitch?'

Jason wasn't scared anymore. He ignored the pain. It was time.

'Yeah,' Jason shouted, 'Give me some more you gay fuck!'

Amine was a little shocked by Jason's words, taken aback, and that was the fraction of a second that Jason needed to make his move.

With all his might, using the energy that remained in his drug-fuelled yet abused body, he freed an arm and grabbed back at the gun, pulling it out of his behind and pushing it away from him and into the mattress, at the same time forcing himself along the bed with his legs as Amine struggled to contain him whilst concentrating on over-powering the hand that Jason had on the barrel of the gun.

In the commotion, Amine sits down on Jason's back, but allows him to wriggle free his other arm.

Amine now concentrated on keeping the gun away from himself, and wrapped his free arm around Jason's throat, squeezing as hard as he could.

But the table had turned again. Jason had the knife in his hand, and stabbed blindly and frantically at the man who straddled him from behind.

He felt and heard the knife make contact. He

felt Amine grow weaker yet heavier on his back. And then he felt the blood flow faster and faster down onto the back of his head and his neck.

Amine stopped struggling, he stopped moving, and then he stopped breathing.

Jason took a few moments to regain his breath, then rolled Amine off his back and got to his feet. He looked at the Arab, dead on the bed, and then at the knife, covered in blood.

He smiled, thoughts ticking over in his head.

He would keep the knife, the knife that saved his life. He wouldn't even clean it. The blood would remind him how valuable it was to him. But he'd leave the gun. There were some things that he would never want reminding of.

He put the knife in his pocket and went to the bathroom to clean up, rinse the blood off his top and out of his hair.

Back in the kitchen, he sealed the bag of Powder and stuck it into his pocket, before shaping the remaining Coke on the work-surface into something that resembled a line and with a few attempts, sniffed it all up.

Nearly twenty minutes had passed, and Jason still hadn't shown his face. This was making me nervous again. I stood up, ready to say 'fuck it' and leave Jason to it, but then I saw him leave the block of apartments and walk in my direction.

'What took you so long?' I asked.

'I found the Charlie,' he said, tapping his pocket and wiping his nose.

'You were ages,' I said, as I started walking alongside him, bag over my shoulder, 'Did Amine wake up?'

'Yeah, he did,' he said.

I stopped, and then Jason stopped and turned back to me.

'Don't worry, you pussy,' he said, pulling out a few of the cable-ties from one of his many pockets, 'He's all tied up.'

'Jesus Christ,' I said, under my breath.

We carried on walking home, happy that the job was done, with occasional thoughts running through my head that I tried my hardest not to think about.

I didn't know how Jason was so unconcerned about Amine catching up with him at a later date, even that very day. But then, as long as I was gone, I wasn't too bothered about it. Jason could look after himself. And even if he couldn't, I didn't care.

Maybe Jason even had plans of his own, to leave or whatever, I just didn't want to know.

24 – GETTING TO THE TRUTH

Jason was sat at the dining table racking up more lines of Cocaine, and drinking beer at a quick rate. He'd nearly finished his third bottle within the half hour we'd been back. I was hoping the alcohol and lack of sleep would force him into his bed, but the Coke was keeping him up, and he didn't look like he wanted any rest.

He was buzzing from finally putting Amine in his place.

'Where the fuck is she?' he said.

He was clearly disturbed that Sarah wasn't there, welcoming him home with open arms, praising him for defeating her bully of an ex-boyfriend and offering herself to him as payment for his services rendered.

I sat at the coffee table, counting the money, confused at how much there seemed to be.

'She's at work,' I answered. 'She'll be home soon.'

He struggled to snort his next line of Coke. His nostrils were getting inflamed and blocked up, and I knew this because I'd been there many times myself.

'How much is meant to be there? Twenty grand?' he asked. 'Is it all there? Did you want some of this?'

He was high as a kite, he couldn't stop twitching his legs and talking nonsense. I'd never seen him this high, or maybe it was that I'd never been sober when he had been like this, and it was the first time I realised how ridiculous he looked and acted when in this state.

'Did I look as stupid as that when on drugs? Another reason to stop,' I thought.

'No, I'm alright,' I said, declining the offer. 'And there's definitely over twenty grand here.'

There was over twenty-thousand euros, way over. Something didn't make sense. I had a sickly feeling in my stomach, was I being cynical or had I been duped?

We heard a key go into the front door so Jason straightened out the shirt he was now wearing, and sat upright in his chair.

'Ready for inspection,' I thought.

I relaxed back into my seat, wishing away the next couple of hours and wanting to be on that flight out of there.

Sarah walked into the front room, dropped her keys and phone on the table next to Jason, and raised her eyebrows when she saw the Charlie and paraphernalia next to him.

'Bit early for that, Jason, no?' she asked, rhetorically.

She turned to say hello to me, but saw the money first and stopped in her tracks for a second or two, before returning to the lying, calculated bitch that I was just discovering her to be.

'You did it,' she said, smiling at me, and patting Jason on the shoulder.

'Anything for you, beautiful,' said Jason, slurring his words.

He sparked a cigarette and started tipping out more Cocaine. Sarah saw that I wasn't over the moon and sat down opposite me on the other sofa. A large stack of cash and an ugly vase separated us.

'Was he home?' she asked. 'I'm a bit worried what he's going to do when he finds out we've taken the money.'

'It's like butter wouldn't melt in her mouth' I thought, staring at her, not sure how to go about the conversation we both knew we were about to have.

'You don't have to worry about Amine,' piped up Jason, 'I'm here for you now, Sarah, and always will be.'

I leant forward in my seat, preparing my words carefully, as I knew that coming across as aggressive to Sarah wouldn't be too clever with her guard dog sat across the room, high and as dangerous as he was, but I didn't like being taken for a ride and manipulated into doing something I didn't want to, even if I had reason to hate Amine, after the kicking he'd organised for me.

I looked her in the eye, then at the money, and then back at her.

I could see that she was surprised by how much cash sat there between us, piled all nice and neatly.

'So how much money did you say there was, Sarah?' I asked, 'Does it look like it's all there?'

Would she come clean? Would she be the good girl who lost her way and admit the truth when confronted with the evidence? Or would she deny any wrong-doing, play dumb and act confused?

'Oh, err, twenty-thousand, give or take,' she said. 'It looks about right. Did you count it?'

I sat back on the couch, for a moment I held my head in my hands, and sighed. She was lying to me, to my face, I hated that.

'Yeah, I counted it,' I said, then looked her in the eye again. 'This is your money isn't it, Sarah?'

She claimed that it was, of course, and only began to buckle when I told her that I'd counted ninety thousand euros. Jason sat at the table, listening in, interested, I don't think that he knew that she had lied, he was too high to really follow proceedings, but he knew that I wasn't happy with her, and clearly that annoyed him. I could hear him shifting in his seat.

I was so close to being away from all of this bullshit, away from all of this trouble and all of these people, but I had a moment of weakness, and instead of letting it go, letting her have her stolen money and leaving her and Jason to their lives, I had to let her know that she had let me down. That I had done this for her, as a friend, and I felt offended by the dishonesty.

'How come you and Amine split up?' I asked, and then continued before she could answer, 'Why did you send us round to steal his money? It is his money isn't it? He's gonna go fucking mental, Sarah. Did he tell you it was only twenty grand because he didn't trust you, thinking you wouldn't fuck him over for that amount? Or was that just a guess because you didn't know how much of his money he had stashed in his bag?'

And then she broke.

First her eyes welled-up, then the first couple of tears made their escape, down her beautiful face before being wiped away by her soft, well-manicured hands.

'He dumped me,' she said, struggling to compose herself, on the edge of breaking down completely, 'he dumped me when I needed him most.'

'Why?' I asked, 'What do you mean?'

I heard Jason crack his knuckles and he sat upright on the edge of his chair, he was ready to go at me. I was upsetting Sarah and he didn't like it one bit.

'Leave her alone, Jimbo,' he said.

But I was also angry over the deceit, and I wanted to know why she did this, to me, and even to Amine. What had changed between them that she would risk his wrath like this? Was it so big that it warranted sending Jason and me to steal from him, risking getting hurt or even prison, maybe both?

'Are you gonna tell us why you need this money so much that you sent us to rob your boyfriend?' I persisted, 'Why didn't he want you anymore?'

Tears were streaming down her face at this point, and when Jason got to his feet and stumbled in our direction, I honestly thought I was about to get another beating.

But he didn't go for me.

He sat down beside Sarah, put his arm around her and tried to comfort her. It was clear that however much he disliked me, even hated me at that moment, he loved Sarah more, even when she didn't reciprocate those feelings.

She pushed away the snotty-nosed, drugged-up fool and he fell to the floor. He stayed down, trying hard get a grip of himself.

I realised just how fucked on the Coke that Jason was at that moment, and although I knew he was still incredibly dangerous, he could hardly lift himself from the floor, his face muscles twitching and straining from the effort. Then he laid flat on his back, trying to regain an ounce of composure.

'So?' I said, turning my attention back to my tearful landlady.

'I'm pregnant, ok? And I told him,' she said, before falling to pieces for a few seconds, then sitting upright and wiping her face. She stared me in the eye, ready to spill the beans.

'But Amine can't have kids, apparently,' she continued, 'so he knows I've been sleeping with someone else. And he left me.'

The news was the shot of adrenaline that Jason needed, it didn't sober him up completely, but he was up on his elbows and able to pay attention to what was going on, to the truths that were unfolding around us.

'So he found out you cheated on him,' I said, not accepting any of the blame for this one, 'and then you sent us around to rob him, what, to get back at him for dumping you?'

I couldn't believe it.

A woman scorned, even when that woman was a long way from innocent herself, could really fuck a man over.

She leant over the table, reached her hands out

over the money that now seemed to be only part of the problem, and tried to take my hands in hers, but I pulled away, to demonstrate that I wanted nothing more to do with this.

'He's gonna go mad,' I continued, 'and I don't blame him.'

'Let's not do this, let's not argue,' she pleaded. 'I love Amine. I never wanted this to happen.'

And then I made a mistake.

'So whose kid is it?' I asked. 'I know it isn't mine, we only fucked a couple of days ago.'

I froze, realising what I'd just done, as I felt Jason's eyes drill a hole into the side of my head. I only dared to look at him, when out of the corner of my eye, I saw him turn his gaze to Sarah, he did not look happy, and then she looked back at me, clearly worried at what was likely about to happen.

Silence filled the room, and the air became too thick to breathe without the sound of inhaling and exhaling echoing off the walls.

25 – THE TRUTH HURTS

Sarah and I could only sit, frozen to the spot, as Jason slowly climbed to his knees, then pushed himself up and stood at the end of the coffee table, looking down on us, distraught from the betrayal that he felt from the pair of us.

He reached into his cargo pants and pulled out a large knife, which he held up to the light to examine it, which is when I saw the dried blood on the blade.

'Oh, fucking hell.'

I looked to Sarah, had she seen the blood? What had he done? Did she know how far Jason would go, and what he was capable of?

I didn't know what to do, other than play the proverbial rabbit in the headlights and await my fate.

And then he spoke, slowly, battling against the Cocaine in his system to take control, to put his message across to us clearly and concisely.

'Firstly,' he said, 'you ain't gotta worry about Amine coming 'round. He's stuck in bed, and he's goin' nowhere.'

'What have you done, Jason?' asked Sarah, the realisation that he may have taken things too far with her beloved Amine, finally dawning on her.

He didn't answer, he didn't need to.

'And secondly,' he continued, turning to me and pointing the tip of the blade towards my face, 'I told you, keep your fucking hands off Sarah.'

He pounced on top of me, forcing me into the corner of the sofa, his free hand on my throat, and jabbing the knife towards my face.

I had hold of both of his wrists, desperately wrestling the hand holding the knife away from me, whilst trying to loosen the grip of the hand that squeezed my windpipe.

His full weight was on me, and as much as I tried to push him and the weapon away from, I couldn't budge him. The nasty, little man was fully-charged and angry, and I just didn't know how to defend myself.

I've read about people saying that they've had their lives flash before their eyes in deadly situations, and that they'd thought about loved ones and had regrets over things they had or hadn't done.

Bollocks.

'Get that fucking knife away from me,' was the only thing going through my mind, nothing else.

'Jason, no,' screamed Sarah.

'You wanna fuck with me, you English cunt?' shouted Jason. 'I'll cut you up, like I did that fuckin' Moroccan.'

I'd managed to get the blade away from my right eye, which is where it was originally heading, but now it was very close to piercing my neck, not that I could see it. I could just feel the tip of it picking at my skin just above the point at where he was strangling me.

The adrenaline was pumping for both us, the testosterone running so high it must have stank the room out, possibly attracting ovulating women from miles around.

His crazy eyes drilled down into mine with so much hate and disgust. Snot fell from his nose onto me, dribble from his mouth down into mine and onto my cheek.

'Stop it, just stop it,' yelled Sarah, who was ignored by Jason.

To me, it sounded like I was underwater when she screamed; such was the pressure on my neck and chest. My ears had popped and all I could clearly hear was my attempts at breathing, the sounds of a man struggling to survive.

The knife was no longer bouncing on and off of my neck, it remained there, constantly touching, millimetre by millimetre, edging its way in and breaking skin.

Jason was winning the fight, and I was about to die.

SMASH

I never knew that the sound of a breaking vase was the most beautiful sound in the world.

Jason slumped down on me, motionless, as pieces of the ugly vase, the gift he had once given to Sarah when in his not-so-subtle way of courting, fell down from the back of his head and landed beside me.

Sarah stood in tears, as broken as the vase itself.

She had saved my life.

I pushed the unconscious murderer to the floor, and he fell with a bump between the sofa and the coffee table.

I took a few deep breaths, composed myself as best I could and stood up, shaking the large shards of broken ceramic from my clothing. I kicked the knife away from his hand and turned to Sarah, in time to see her collapse to her knees, clinging to the sofa for dear life.

'I'm sorry, I'm so sorry.' she repeated.

I looked back at Jason, comprehending the seriousness of his actions, of our actions, and knew I had to act fast.

The shit had well and truly hit the fan. The only way out of this mess was to disappear and never look back. That sounded ok to me.

'He killed Amine, Sarah,' I said, finding it hard to believe I was saying these words about someone I'd been calling a friend, a mate. 'He's fucking stabbed him to death.'

I looked over at the table where Jason had been sitting, the Charlie, a rolled up note, and his bank card were next to Sarah's keys and phone, along with the cable-ties from earlier.

I had an idea.

I approached the table and checked that Sarah wasn't looking as I slipped her phone into my pocket. I picked up the cable-ties and went back to Jason and Sarah watched as I yanked his hands behind his back and tied him up. I then attached a couple of ties around his ankles for good measure. Then I gave him a couple of punches to the side of his face, partly to keep him unconscious for longer, partly out of spite.

I turned back to Sarah, who was still on hers knees, motionless, and silent except from the sniffling.

'We've got to call the police, Sarah,' I said, softly.

She shook her head.

I moved beside her, fell to my knees, and face to face with her, placed my hands lightly on her shoulders.

'Sarah, he's killed Amine,' I said. 'And we've stolen his money.'

'I can't,' she said, shaking her head again.

'I'm not going to jail for this, I thought I was doing you a favour,' I said. 'We've got to pin it on Jason. He's the psychopath here. You've got to call the Old Bill, Sarah.'

'No,' she said, adamant now, coming out of the shock of what she had just seen and heard, 'I can't send him to jail.'

'What? Why the fuck not?' I asked, growing impatient, the adrenaline still pulsing through my body. 'You're gonna have a kid, Sarah. Do you want someone like him around your baby?'

'It's Jason's baby,' she snapped, looking my deep in the eyes, and I knew that it wasn't a lie.

She fell towards me, buried her head in my neck and started sobbing again.

I was stunned.

So he had been having his way with her, the little bastard. No wonder he got so jealous. I wondered how long it had been going on, until I realised that I didn't actually give a shit.

I took her by the shoulders and gently peeled her away from me.

'Listen, someone is going to prison,' I said, 'and it's not going to be me. So tell me, is it gonna be you?'

She shook her head again, but this time it was the response that I wanted.

'No,' she said, wiping away the tears from her cheeks.

'You phone the cops, and I'll keep an eye on him,' I said.

Slowly she stood, got her bearings and went to the table and threw her hands up in despair, before checking the coffee table and saying that she must have left her phone at the bar.

'Go and get mine,' I said, 'it's in my room.'

As she went to get my phone, I quickly went through Jason's pockets and found his phone, pulled out the battery and slipped the parts under the sofa.

Sarah came back into the front room with my phone in her hand.

'It doesn't work,' she said, frustrated.

'Oh shit,' I said, already knowing that to be the case. 'I forgot. It got busted last night.'

I tapped on Jason's pockets, feigning a search for his phone then shook my head as I gave up looking.

'You'll have to go and find the police outside, they're always floating around, I said. 'Quick as you can.'

I was taking control of the situation, and I was so happy to be sober at this point, I could only imagine how much I would have been flapping if I was high or hung-over.

Yes, I was in a pickle, to say the least, but I was clear-headed and knew what had to be done.

I took Sarah in my arms, wiped her fresh tears

away and spoke calmly. I told her that I'd protect her, that we'd get through this together, and that doing this to Jason was the best thing for him, that maybe he could rebuild a new future when he'd paid for his crimes.

We quickly agreed a plan.

Sarah reluctantly left the apartment in search of the police, leaving me to guard Jason and clear away the Charlie from the table and hide the money, just leaving our killer, and his finger prints all over the murder weapon for the police to use as evidence.

But as soon as I heard the door close behind her, I put a different plan into action.

I picked up my broken phone from the table and stuck it in my pocket. Swiftly moving to my room, I dug out my passport and stuck it in my back pocket, then zipped up the packed suitcase and dumped it by the front door.

I ran back to the front room and packed up most of the money into the sports bag. I left Sarah about twenty thousand on the coffee table. That's what she originally asked for, right?

Back in the bedroom for one last check, all clear. Then I was into the bathroom for my toothbrush and razor. The front room again, looking for anything of mine.

Nothing remained that would indicate I'd ever been in the apartment, except fingerprints and DNA, but I didn't have time to wipe everything down.

'This'll have to do.'

Jason started to regain consciousness, so I

stood above and said goodbye. I told him that it was nice knowing him, before bringing my foot down on his head.

It was time to go.

26 – IT'S ESCAPE FOR SOME

Walking along the sea-front with my suitcase and the sports bag, I probably looked like any other tourist, except maybe for my cuts and bruises.

Occasionally I would have to pass the police, and sometimes the 'Guardia Civil', who were just like the police, but on steroids. This of course made me nervous, but all I could do was keep on walking, find a taxi and go.

At one point, a police car drove slowly past me, and the officer in the passenger seat gave me a long, hard stare. Of course, by this time, it was possible that Sarah was back at the apartment with the police and found that I had gone, and maybe they had a description out on me.

To get out of view, I approached a market stand with a few people gathered around. I then had the idea of changing my appearance, and bought a baseball cap and a T-shirt; the top had the words 'Costa Del Soldier' printed across the front, and I thought this was very apt. I put it on and dumped the top I took off into a bin.

I called out to an approaching taxi but the driver ignored me. As he passed I saw it was the driver from the night before. He really didn't take a shine to me, that guy.

Cap on, I was ready to move again.

Sarah, already stressed, led two policemen into her apartment. Her stress levels rose more so as she followed the armed policemen into the front room.

Nobody else was there.

Sarah had explained the situation to the policemen in their own language, without a problem, but at this point they questioned her ability to speak the lingo as what she had said was clearly not the case.

There wasn't anybody there, not a murderer tied up on the floor, or another man watching over him. But there was a bloody knife, sat next to piles of cash on the coffee table. And there was also 'Cocaina' on the main table.

Things were far from what Sarah had told the police they would find in the apartment, and she had some serious explaining to do, although first, she was handcuffed, sat down and had a gun drawn on her by one of the officers, whilst the other searched the apartment.

Robbo stood beside his red Ferrari at a petrol garage, the petrol hose filling the tank, as he talked on his mobile phone.

A young member of staff, Juan, was sent out by the manager of the garage to tell Robbo that the use of a mobile phone was strictly prohibited, and that he had to end the call straight away.

Robbo said he didn't understand Spanish, in Spanish, and said he didn't take too kindly to being nagged at by a mere kiosk worker. The employee was then ignored, until the petrol tank was full, the fuel cover locked and Robbo had finished his phone call.

Juan had remained calm and professional throughout, asking him politely, in Spanish and broken English, to hang up the phone, but was clearly stressed as his manager looked on and he hadn't been able to get the arrogant Englishman to comply in a timely manner.

Robbo stared the young Juan in the eye. He then took out his wallet, opened it up, and showed him a large wad of cash before he walked past him towards the kiosk window to pay. It was probably twice the amount that Juan earned in a month.

He was a cruel bastard, Robbo.

He joined the queue, checked his watch and grew impatient at having to wait for those few precious seconds.

But then gladly, things got worse for Robbo. Karma, some might say.

The engine of the red Ferrari started up with a roar and pulled away and out of the garage forecourt. Robbo came running but slipped in his expensive shoes, landing heavily on his knee in a puddle of grease, his phone falling into pieces as it made contact with the ground.

He looked up, desperately searching for someone to help him. The only one person near was Juan.

'That's my car, called out Robbo. 'That's my fucking car. Call the police, call the fucking police.'

'No comprendo, señor,' replied Juan, a little smile on his face.

There were now four police officers with Sarah at her apartment, and after a load of photos had been taken, the money, the knife and the Powder had been bagged up.

Jason hadn't cleaned his room out before he left; he'd just grabbed a few things.

The police didn't know exactly what the story was at this point, and they didn't think to look and see if he had taken his passport. They had no doubt that a man was also living in the apartment with Sarah, but in reality, so far, all they had was an hysterical woman, drugs, money and a weapon that she had previously stated was used to murder her boyfriend.

Sarah knew how bad this must have looked, and when one of the officers took a call that confirmed a dead body with knife wounds, and a shitty-smelling gun had been found at the address she had given them, the gravity of the situation sank in.

Sarah broke down in tears again; between the crying and the heat of the morning, she must have been close to dehydration.

'I told you, I haven't done anything wrong, please let me go,' she pleaded, as two of the officers led her out of the apartment. 'There were two men here, they killed my boyfriend. Please, please let me go.'

I was in a toilet cubicle in the airport, aware of the irony that my great escape from a life of drugs was partly taking place in a preferred location for taking drugs.

I transferred the money from the sports bag into my suitcase, the checking-in document that I'd printed into my trouser pockets, and then checked all of my pockets, making sure I had everything I needed, and nothing that I didn't.

I found a bag of Coke, deep down in the corner of my pocket, and I thought about how many people I knew who'd think that finding a gram would be a stroke of luck. And I guess I did as well, but for different reasons, as being caught going through security with that in my pocket would have potentially caused me all manner of problems.

I studied the little bag in my hand, tore it open and inspected the Charlie. This used to be a God to me, the joy in my day, and my energy at night, it was what my days were built around.

I moved my suitcase off of the toilet, opened the lid, and tipped out the Cocaine. The Powder fell to the water. It was like watching snowflakes disappear into a lake.

I was ready to go.

The last hurdle in my escape was getting checked-in and going through security.

'This shouldn't be a problem,' I was telling myself. Sarah didn't know my last name, bizarrely, after all these months, and I didn't think Jason would be in a position to point the finger. Plus neither of them knew that I had booked a flight, so I figured I had time on my side. Of course, the closer I came to check-in, and then security, the more the nerves began to play up.

But then I was through. I was on the home

straight, and I didn't have long before I was due to board the flight, so I bought a newspaper and a bottle of water, and headed to the boarding gate.

Sarah was at the Marbella police station, no longer in her own clothes, but wearing a tatty gown that had been issued to her by a female officer, who then to follow procedures, gave Sarah a cavity search.

She felt utterly humiliated as she was led off to have her fingerprints and mug shots taken.

I switched on my mp3 player, put in the earphones, and took my time looking over the menu as I sat in my window seat. Nothing really appealed, it was a budget airline, but I opted for a bacon roll anyway. On a full stomach, I could maybe sleep for an hour or so.

The relief that washed over me as we first took off and I saw the sea below me hadn't subsided. I was happy and I was free.

I'd learnt some valuable lessons in Spain, lessons that would stay with me forever. Yes, I'd hit rock bottom in some respects, but I was two days clean, and going back to rehab first thing when touching down in England.

I couldn't wait to see my family, and tell my mum how sorry I was for the past, and that I was finally ready to be someone who brought happiness into her life, not misery and stress.

I felt bad for leaving Sarah to deal with the police on her own, but she lied to me, to everyone about everything, as far as I could now tell.

I had figured out that Sarah saw getting

pregnant would keep Amine for life, even get the marriage proposal from him that she so clearly desired. But her plan, to get pregnant by any means necessary, such as shagging a junkie like me and a psycho like Jason, backfired because Amine fired blanks.

After all the charm and class I thought she displayed, she was just a desperate woman looking for love in the wrong places, scheming deviously without giving a damn about the consequence, and which in this case, caused the death of the man she loved.

And that leaves Jason looking at a lengthy jail term. Although to be honest, locking him up is probably the best thing for everyone, except him.

As I drifted off to sleep, I remember feeling happy and confident about the future, for the first time in a long time.

'All my troubles are behind me.'

At the back of the plane, a small child dropped his toy car to the floor, and with his seatbelt on, he wasn't able to pick it back up. The helpful, young man beside him, sat on the aisle seat and wearing sunglasses, scooped it up and handed it back to him.

'Say "thank you," Charlie,' said the boy's mother.

'Thank you, mister,' said the boy, looking up at the broad grin on the kind stranger.

'No worries mate,' said the Australian. 'And what a good name you've got. I do like that name, Charlie.'

GET CLEAN

THE END

A word from Jams N. Roses…

Thank you for taking the time to finish this book. I hope you enjoyed the reading as much as I did the writing. On the following pages are details of my other titles, I hope you find something that peaks your interest.

I am an independent author, and my only hope of success in this business is by news of my work spreading by word of mouth. A short, positive review left on Amazon would help me immensely, and would also be truly appreciated. So, if you enjoyed this book, <u>please leave a positive comment on Amazon.</u>

Thank you.

Also available now on Amazon...

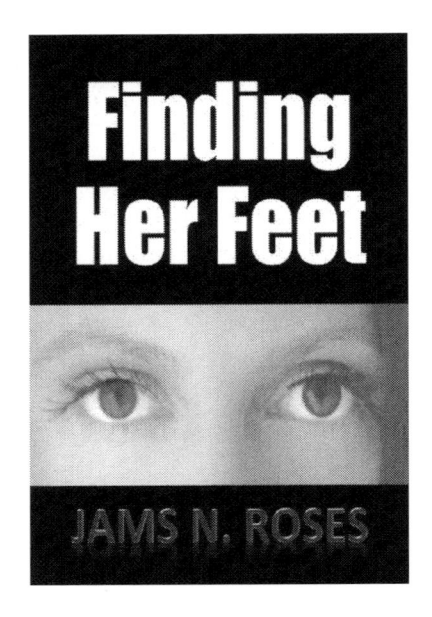

Finding Her Feet – Drama. Tragedy. Family. Life.

The tragedy begins as Amanda watches her sister fall through the broken ice. Heartbreakingly, Samantha doesn't reappear until the following day, when her lifeless body is pulled from the water. The devastation continues as the family falls apart under the weight of emotional pain and unfair blame.

When overwhelmed with guilt, how does a child cope with a death in the family?

Also available now on Amazon...

Son of a Serial Killer

Ben Green is a troubled young man, losing his mind and hearing voices. Worse than that, his nightmare is just beginning...

Detective Inspector Summers hates dealing with drug addicts, thieves, violent men and women, rapists, child molesters and murderers. She wants to be a doctor in a surgery, saving the lives of the sick. Instead, she deals with the sick and twisted.

Finally, she gets handed the case she wants, the reason she joined the force... Her investigations lead Summers closer to Ben, and his involvement to the case slowly becomes clear...

Also available now on Amazon...

Blood of a Serial Killer - Murder in the Genes Book 2

The bloodline continues..

It's only natural for Benny Jones to want to know more about the father he never met. He's turning eighteen and so his doting mother, Eve, can no longer put off answering his questions because he is too young to understand.

Discovering whose genes he carries, Benny grasps why he has behaved the way he has in recent times and is intrigued to learn more about the darker side of his family. He has so many questions, and his grandmother Lily Green, once known as the notorious killer The Phantom, lives on in a mental hospital not far from home and she could supply the answers.

The corpses pile up as Benny discovers his purpose in life...

JAMS N. ROSES

Also available now on Amazon...

Fanatic - Murder in the Genes Book 3

What would your hero do?
FANATIC...
Martin Day is at breaking point. The loner, ignored and ridiculed for as long as he can remember, looks to his hero for inspiration. Sadly, for those in the near vicinity, the person Martin looks up to most is notorious killer The Phantom.

Also available now on Amazon…

The Infidel Soldiers

In the year 2020, Britain is great no more. Political correctness, denial and apathy enabled the most aggressive of beliefs to claim power over what was once a nation of free speech, free will and democracy...

William White, a soldier injured on tour whilst serving his country in Syria, has seen the drastic changes in his homeland and knows the battle of ideologies is no longer worth fighting; the war has already been lost. Then one day, out of the blue, Joe Taylor crashes into William's life and demands the ex-soldier helps him fight the good fight.

The two men show each other what is important in life; what is worth fighting for, and what is worth dying for. They are two very different men who had both given up hope, but then they became the infidel soldiers...

Also available now on Amazon...

<u>Extremely England</u>

Thank you for buying this satirical and farcical comedy.

Unless of course you haven't, and you're one of those people who hops from book cover to blurb and back again, only to wander off without purchasing what could quite possibly have been the first book in ages to really make you laugh!

If that's the case, then take the leap of faith. Put your proverbial hand in your pocket, click the 'buy now with 1 click' button and get involved.

Why? Because 'Extremely England' is a naughty novella full of farcical fun! Let's laugh at modern day England, because if not, we're likely to cry.

Contains rude and crude humour - Not for the easily offended!

Printed in Great Britain
by Amazon